I AM
THE PROMISE KEEPER

I AM The Promises Keeper
Copyright © 2022 by Brad Wyrick

Published in the United States of America

ISBN   Paperback: 978-1-957312-93-4
ISBN   Hardback: 978-1-958030-88-2
ISBN   eBook: 978-1-957312-94-1

All rights reserved. No part of this publication may be reproduced, stored in a retrieval system or transmitted in any way by any means, electronic, mechanical, photocopy, recording or otherwise without the prior permission of the author except as provided by USA copyright law.

The opinions expressed by the author are not necessarily those of ReadersMagnet, LLC.

ReadersMagnet, LLC
10620 Treena Street, Suite 230 | San Diego, California, 92131 USA
1.619. 354. 2643 | www.readersmagnet.com

Book design copyright © 2022 by ReadersMagnet, LLC. All rights reserved.

Cover design by Ericka Obando
Interior design by Daniel Lopez

I AM
THE PROMISE KEEPER

"For all the promises of God in Him are Yes, and in Him Amen, to the glory of God through us."

(2 Corinthians 1:20)

Follow Me - Book One

Brad Wyrick

TABLE OF CONTENTS

Introduction ix

Chapter 1	"I Am That I Am" 1
Chapter 2	Broken Promises 20
Chapter 3	Liar-Liar, Pants On Fire.. 35
Chapter 4	I Am The Promise-Keeper 45
Chapter 5	Don't Cherry Pick The Tree Of Life 53
Chapter 6	The Short Cut Lie Is Quid Pro Quo............................ 62
Chapter 7	The Empty Nets Of Success.. 82
Chapter 8	Praying Scripture Empowers our Prayer Life............. 89
Chapter 9	More Precious Than Gold... 98
Chapter 10	God's Still Small Voice...105

About The Author...111

I dedicate this book to the GREAT I AM
who died for me. I love You, Jesus.

INTRODUCTION: I AM THE PROMISE KEEPER

"I AM that I AM"

"God's promises will expire (in the twinkling of an eye) between our last breath and our entrance into eternity."

I don't know about you, but I get a few gift cards throughout the year. There is always some celebration awaiting the turning of the calendar month. Back in the dark ages, I received shirts and ties, but now it's the free stack of gift cards awaiting their redemption.

God's promises are a lot like gift cards that are left unused. He has made a lot of promises to us, and we need to take hold of those promises. If you think about it, Christmas has a lot to do with guarantees.

Going back to the very beginning, God promised Adam and Eve that a Deliverer would come one day. God pledged to Isaiah that a virgin would conceive and give birth to the

Savior. And God promised Mary she would give birth to that Savior. The angel Gabriel even affirmed this, saying, "For the word of God will never fail" (Luke 1:37 NLT).

God wants us to know that He keeps His promises. He certainly kept His promise with Mary, and she was surprised and humbled that God chose her.

Sometimes I'll come across a gift card that I forgot about for a place I like. I'm excited to discover that I have that gift card. I'm also amazed that I haven't used it yet.

Like God's gifts, they're just sitting there in the Bible, waiting for us to take hold and apply them to our life. But if we don't read the Word, we won't know God's promises. We need to read them, believe them, apply them, and start living these promises out.

GOD FULFILLS HIS PROMISES

God has made many promises that He intends to keep. They are not without action on our part. Designed to bless us, assuming we meet His conditions. Those seeking to utilize any promise should be Seeking Him, Walking with Him, Living in Him, and Obeying Him.

There are over 3,000 promises in the Bible and finding one for any need is possible with God's guidance. However, we must believe in faith that God will fulfill His promises.

Then we apply the principles of scripture to receive the benefits of His blessings. It is not enough to read a promise, name it and claim it, expecting God to apply it in your life. Promises are not God's "Blab It and Grab It Doctrine"! God doesn't play that game!

GOD WILL MOVE HEAVEN AND EARTH TO BLESS YOU

God's omnipotent power behind His Promises and Principles cannot be stopped by human force. Nothing on this earth or in the universe, whether visible or invisible, can prevent what God has promised for those who are His children. His promises are sure and true. If God wants to bless you, nothing will hinder His blessings. "What then shall we say to these things? If God is for us, who can be against us?" (Romans 8:31).

We can trust in them, lean upon them, apply them, and have the assurance that what God promises, He delivers through His effectual power to bring to pass all that His Word proclaims. It was by His Word that the universe came into existence, "For he spoke, and it came to be; he commanded, and it stood firm" (Psalm 33:9), and "we understand that the universe was created by the Word of God" (Hebrews 11:3).

Absolute belief in God's Word is mandatory for every believer. Jesus is dead serious about His Word; in fact, He died to keep His Word. We so often try to assemble something without the owner's manual. God, in His divine wisdom, has supplied us instructions within the pages of scripture. Who better to teach us than the author and finisher of our faith (Jesus) in all doctrinal truths?

Believing our Lord has a divine purpose behind every promise will help us to respond based upon scriptural truth and not our feelings. With every Promise brings opportunities and responsibilities. God is more concerned about our character than our comfort. His goal is not to pamper us physically but to perfect us spiritually.

Jesus Christ declared, "I have come. In the volume of the book, it is written of Me." Therefore, Scripture should always be at the threshold of every decision we face. For it is God's Mind Written Down. It's like Jesus reciting Himself.

In human terms, promises are easily broken. In God's terms, they are a sure thing. Knowing what God has promised us and how he keeps his promises gives us assurance, hope, and peace.

May God lead you to discover the promises He intended for your life. Might God's Word bless you, keep you, and be a light unto your path.

1

"I AM THAT I AM"

Then I said, "Behold, I have come—In the volume of the book it is written of Me—To do Your will, O God" (Hebrews 10:7).

Life was so simple back when I was a child with all my heroes, all my cartoons, all my favorite shows. It's incredible how eventually my heroes let me down. When childhood heroes let you down, look up, and see Jesus.

I was delighted when MIGHTY MOUSE hit the TV Screen singing, "Mr. trouble never hangs around, when he hears this Mighty sound, Here I come to save the day! That means that Mighty Mouse is on the way..."

Well, eventually, I figured out that a Mighty Mouse couldn't save any of my days. However, it was fun while it lasted.

Then, of course, we have POPEYE THE SAILOR MAN, otherwise known as the Great Spinach Conspiracy.

"I'm Popeye the Sailor Man. I'm strong to the finich, cause I eats me spinach. I'm Popeye the Sailor Man…"

I would flex in front of the mirror after each portion of that green stuff. Never looking like the bodybuilder promised, I lost all faith in this guy

I would be remorse if I didn't mention SUPERMAN. This guy was faster than a speeding bullet, more powerful than a locomotive, able to leap tall buildings in a single bound. Discovering that Clark Kent and Superman were the same, my inner soul was dashed to its core.

I didn't get it! All he had to do was remove his glasses, and he became a superhero. And no one at the newspaper or around the world knew he was just Clark Kent without glasses.

Yes. It's Superman, strange visitor from another planet who came to Earth with powers and abilities far beyond those of mortal men. Superman, who can change the course of mighty rivers, bend steel with his bare hands, and who, disguised as Clark Kent, mild-mannered reporter for a great metropolitan newspaper, fights a never-ending battle for truth, justice, and the American way.

Yea, RIGHT!

One of my greatest disappointments was when BAMBI died at the end of the movie. I think this was the first time I had a good cry without being spanked. What a bummer, this precious little dear gets bumped off, and it tore me up.

One good thing happened on the way to eternity. I came to realize that JESUS WAS THE REASON FOR THE SEASON, so I dropped Santa Claus like a bad habit.

"When I was a child, I spoke as a child, I understood as a child, I thought as a child; but when I became a man, I put away childish things. For now, we see in a mirror dimly, but then face to face. Now I know in part, but then I shall know just as I also am known. And now abide faith, hope, love, these three; but the greatest of these is love" (1 Corinthians 13:11-13).

"I AM THAT I AM"

The mighty God of the universe calls Himself I AM. In Exodus 3:14, the Bible says, "And God said unto Moses, I AM THAT I AM." Moses had said, "When I go down to Egypt, and the people ask me who sent me, what shall I tell them." God said, "You tell them that I AM sent you."

WHAT IS THIS I AM? I AM all you will ever need. I AM to you whatever your need may be. And it is interesting, as God declared, "I AM," He was speaking of that eternal aspect of His character. He is the Eternal One.

The angel of the waters announced Him "as the One who is and who was and who is to be," all at once (Revelation 16:5).

Now, with God, there is no past; there is no future; it's all now. He dwells in the eternal. I can't conceive that. But with God, He resides in the infinite currently. "I AM WHO I AM has sent you," describes the eternal characteristic of God.

The name of God is a verb "to be." "The Becoming One" is named Yahweh, as God becomes to you whatever your need might be. "I am your peace, your strength, your help. I am your guide. I am your righteousness. I am your salvation. I am your hope." How beautiful that is. "The Becoming One is named Yahweh, The Becoming One," as God becomes to you whatever your need might be.

By studying the many "I Am" statements interwoven throughout God's Word, specifically, the seven "I Am" statements of Jesus contained in the Gospel of John will reveal His Lordship. All of which points back to the Old Testament and into the kingdom. Thus, proving that Jesus is God and was the God of both the Old and New Testaments.

Understanding how these sayings effects our life will help in applying the truths of scripture. We find every purpose, truth, promise, principle, and provision needed about life eternal. Thus, inspiring the reader, "To know Him and make Him known."

Jesus Christ declared, "I have come. In the volume of the book, it is written of Me." Therefore, Scripture should always be at the threshold of every decision we face because the Bible Is God's Mind Written Down. It's like Jesus reciting Himself.

Everyone probably asks the question, "Who am I, Lord, that I should be the one to do this?" We must have a sense of our unworthiness in being an instrument through which God might do His work. Humble yourself in the sight of the Lord and He will lift you up.

The Apostle Paul acknowledged that ancient Israel "all drank the same spiritual drink. For they drank from the spiritual Rock that followed them, and the Rock was Christ" (1 Corinthians 10:4), which explains why Jesus could authoritatively say, "Truly, truly, I say to you, before Abraham was, I am" (John 8:58). So, Jesus was before Abraham. Like us, there was a time when Abraham did not exist, so Jesus directly tells them (and us) He existed before Abraham, therefore by application, He must be God (and He is!).

Learning what God's Word says about His promises found in each, I AM statement, will help develop our maturity. And, believing our Lord has a divine purpose will help us to respond based upon scripture and not our feelings. Furthermore, you can consider each of His I AM statements as promises. Just believe, receive and apply.

"I AM THE BREAD OF LIFE"

Jesus contrasted himself with the manna that came down from heaven in the time of Moses. The manna provided temporary miraculous substance for the people, as Jesus had just done by feeding the 5000 people. But physical substance is not what people ultimately need. If you eat bread today, you'll need it again tomorrow. Jesus, as the Bread of Life, would fill their spiritual hunger eternally.

When God revealed Himself to Moses, He identified Himself as the "I AM." Now Jesus said, "I AM the bread of life." Your fathers did eat manna in the wilderness, and they are dead. But this is the bread which comes down from heaven, that a man may eat thereof, and not die (John 6:48-50).

The crowds followed Him, but not for the right reason, so He told them, "you are seeking me, not because you saw signs, but because you ate your fill of the loaves" (John 6:26). They only wanted more bread for their stomach, so Jesus said, "Do not work for the food that perishes, but for the food that endures to eternal life, which the Son of Man will give to you. For on him God the Father has set his seal" (John 6:27), and "I am the bread of life; whoever comes to me shall not hunger, and whoever believes in me shall never thirst" (John 6:35), so "All that the Father gives me will come to me, and whoever comes to me I will never cast out" (John 6:37). That is bread unto eternal life.

Jesus fed the physically hungry. But Jesus' most significant concern was for people with spiritual hunger. Bread in the Bible is the symbol of spiritual life. People all over the world are the same; they have an inborn hunger for something, and that something is Christ. People cannot be satisfied with anything less than Christ.

To receive Christ into your heart seems so simple. You open your heart and say, "Lord Jesus, come in. I'm willing to turn from my sins and receive You as my Lord and Savior." Jesus says, "I am the bread of life. He who comes to Me shall never hunger" (John 6:35). This bread satisfies the inner longings and pangs of hunger of the human heart. Have you taken of that bread? You must repent of your sins, change your mind, turn your back on sin and receive Jesus Christ as your Lord and Savior.

"I AM THE LIGHT OF THE WORLD"

With the Pharisees and other religious leaders there, Jesus said, "I am the light of the world. Whoever follows me will not walk in darkness but will have the light of life" (John 8:12). For those who don't believe, whether they realize it or not, they are walking in darkness, and in the ways of their father the Devil, however, such were we too. The light of Christ brings us out of the darkness and into the light, and for those who believe, they will no longer walk in darkness.

Jesus healed the sight of the blind in different ways. One time He used clay. "While I am in the world, I am the light of the world. And when he has thus spoken, he spat on the ground, and made clay of the spittle, and he anointed the eyes of the blind man with the clay" (John 9:5-6).

Believe it or not, it was against their law, the traditional interpretation of it, to make clay on the Sabbath day. However, when He made this clay, He rubbed it in the guy's eyes.

This story reminds me of the time my dog had cancer and was on a special diet. We boiled chicken for her to replace the treats that almost killed her earlier. Once I set the timer, the countdown began. Of course, being the queen of the house, she would use her different barks during the process. Each time she would bark I would tell her, "You got to let it cook, Puppy Girl." When that was done, it had to cool down. I would say to her, "You're not the boss of me; I am the boss of you." My favorite was, "You don't tell me, I tell you." Jesus was telling the Pharisees, "You don't tell me." "I will show you."

When God created the universe, He put the sun a precise distance from the earth. If the sun were a few kilometers closer to us, we would fry. If it were farther from us, we would freeze to death. What the sun is to the earth, Jesus Christ is to the human heart. Jesus said, "I am the light of the world. He who follows Me shall not walk in darkness but have the light of life" (John 8:12).

Scripture also says you have a soul, a spirit living inside of you. When you die, your body goes to the grave. But the spirit, the real you, lives on forever. Jesus said if you come to Him, you will live with Him. Jesus Christ is the One that brings peace in our hearts. He turns His light on in our hearts and is the light to our path.

Ps..., All dogs go to heaven.

"I AM THE DOOR"

I Am the Door, or the Good Shepherd could both apply to John 10:7, where Jesus says, in speaking about His sheep, "I am the door of the sheep" (John 10:7). He guards the door to the sheep pen, by lying down at the door, as shepherds used to (and some still) do. That's why He says, "I am the door. If anyone enters by me, he will be saved and will go in and out and find pasture" (John 10:9). No one gets in the pen without going through the door, and that door is Jesus Christ.

Every building I've ever been to has an entrance somewhere. The Kingdom of God also has an entry. It is Jesus Christ. Jesus was probably familiar with doors because He was the son of a carpenter. A building may have many entries, but God has only one entrance to His Kingdom, and that door is Jesus Christ.

Jesus' statement here shows the importance of the door. "I am the door." If a man tries to come by any other system, by any other way, he's a thief and a robber. Jesus said, "I'm the way, I'm the door. There's one way into the sheepfold, that's through the door.

Try to climb over the walls or whatever, that's the action of a thief and a robber. If you try to enter the kingdom of heaven by your good works, if you decide to enter the kingdom of heaven by being religious, you'll never make it. Jesus said, "I am the way, the truth, and the life, and no man comes to the Father but by Me."

The door swings both ways: "Behold, I stand at the door, and knock: if any man hears my voice, and open the door, I will come into him, and will sup with him, and he with me. To him that overcometh will I grant to sit with me in my throne, even as I also overcame, and am set down with my Father in his throne. He that hath an ear, let him hear what the Spirit saith unto the churches" (Revelation 3:20-22).

"I AM THE GOOD SHEPHERD"

"All we like sheep have gone astray; we have turned everyone to his own way; and the LORD hath laid on him the iniquity of us all" (Isaiah 53:6).

Shortly after saying He was the door, He then adds, "I am the good shepherd. The good shepherd lays down his life for the sheep" (John 10:11). The sheep are helpless without the shepherd because the shepherd leads them to green pastures, leads them to still waters (Psalm 23) because sheep are easily frightened by moving water, but this Shepherd says willingly, "I lay down my life for the sheep."

The sheep know the voice of their Shepherd. There can be many different flocks, all mixed in the fold or at the watering troughs. But when each Shepherd gets up and calls to his sheep, the sheep know their Shepherds voice, and they follow. The sheep feel secure when they are with their Shepherd. And we, as children of God, are protected in Jesus, our Good Shepherd. We are safe in the hand of the Father, and no one can snatch us out of His hand.

The shepherd would sleep in front of that entrance of the sheepfold. Thus, making himself the door and protecting the herd from wolves, wind, and storms. Jesus is our Shepherd, protecting us from Satan.

Jesus tells the story of a lost sheep. This farmer had 99 safe sheep, but one had wandered away. He was lost. So, this shepherd decided that he was going to go after the one lost sheep. After much searching, he found the sheep. And he called all of his friends together, and they rejoiced because he had found the sheep.

Are you that one lost sheep? Jesus Christ would have died on the cross if you were the only one lost. God loves you, and He's searching for you.

The shepherd lives with his sheep. He gives them food and protection and security. Jesus said, "I am with you always, even to the end of the age" (Matthew 28:20). Whatever happens, however sick you may get–you may lose a child, you may lose a father or a mother–Jesus is with you.

You're the sheep; He's the shepherd. He loves you, and He gave His life for you.

But how do I know if I am one of his sheep? How do I know if I am secure? Are you listening to His voice and following Him? If so, then you are one of His sheep.

"I AM THE RESURRECTION, AND THE LIFE"

Since Jesus raised people from the dead, He could say with authority, "I am the resurrection and the life. Whoever believes in me, though he die, yet shall he live, and everyone who lives and believes in me shall never die. Do you believe this?" (John 11:25-26)

Martha was upset because her brother Lazarus had died, and she was blaming Jesus by saying that if Jesus had been there, he would not have died. And if Jesus had been there, He apparently would have just healed Lazarus.

In the Jewish culture, the depth of the love for the deceased was demonstrated by the amount of mourning, even to the point of hiring professional mourners.

Yet Jesus had something more significant in mine. He then made this radical statement, "I am the resurrection and the life. He who believes in Me though he may die he shall live. And whosoever lives and believes in Me shall never die." He was talking about spiritual death, that eternal separation from God. Something that we will never experience.

Death seems to be an opportunity for a natural man to blame God. Death is the result of man's sin. However, the moment believers die, they move out of this earthly body and into an incorruptible body.

He went on to prove what He was saying by showing His authority over physical death. He broke the laws of nature and brought Lazarus back to life. By believing in Him, we know that we will never experience separation from God. He is the resurrection and the life.

Martha and Mary, Lazarus' sisters, found this statement to be accurate, even though Jesus was speaking of those who have eternal life by believing in Him. After this life and death, they will, and we who trust in Christ will live again. Jesus has been asking this question for over 2,000 years; "Do you believe this?"

The raising of Lazarus from the grave is an example of what Jesus can do for us spiritually. We can become new creatures by being born again of the Spirit. God's gift is ours by faith in the works of the cross. What say you?

"I AM THE WAY, THE TRUTH, AND THE LIFE"

Jesus rules out every other religious system. He isn't "a" way but "the" only way to the Father. Thomas said unto him, Lord, we don't know where you're going; and how can we know the way? Jesus said unto him, I am the way, the truth, and the life: no man comes to the Father, but by me (John 14:5-6).

He is declaring He is not one of many ways, but the one and only way. He is also "the truth," not "a truth," and "not a way but the way to life eternal."

The greatest and most deceptive lie conceived by man is that "ALL ROADS LEAD TO GOD." This eternally destructive lie states that since God is love, and you're a good person, God will never send you to hell. The whole and complete truth is, that all roads do lead to God but for distinct reasons and different ends: believers for their rewards and non-believers for judgment.

Furthermore, God doesn't send anyone to hell. We alone choose between heaven or hell according to our belief in or rejection of Jesus Christ. Those who accepted Jesus as their Lord and Savior will receive eternal life. Those who deny Christ will be judged, and by that decision alone, be separated from God for all eternity. Free choice can either be a gift or a curse. Recall the Fall in the Garden and stay obedient to God's Truth.

So, here again, is one of those radical statements of Jesus Christ. "I am the way, the truth, and the life, and no man comes to the Father but by Me." Here, Jesus is declaring that He is the only way by which a man may come to the Father.

The Holy Spirit draws us to the Father. He will use an incident in your life to speak to you. It may be when you're quietly meditating or thinking. Or it may be when you're walking down the street with thousands of people. Amid all those people, God can speak to you. He uses the Holy Spirit to convict people of their need of God.

He draws us. He urges us to receive His Son, Jesus Christ, as the fulfillment of our life, the One who can forgive our sins, the One who can give us eternal life. Have you made that commitment?

Finally, Jesus says He is the life, meaning He is the resurrection and the life. We can read about Lazarus and know that it is true. Jesus was the only way to life for Lazarus, and that's the truth, because there is no other way than through Jesus to receive eternal life. Do you believe this?

"I AM THE VINE"

"Abide in me, and I in you. As the branch cannot bear fruit of itself, except it abide in the vine; no more can ye, except ye abide in me.

I am the vine; ye are the branches: He that abideth in me, and I in him, the same bringeth forth much fruit: for without me ye can do nothing" (John 15:4-5).

The whole purpose in our life is that of being fruitful. The primary desire of my life is to bear good fruit for my

Lord. No other accomplishments that I may achieve are as crucial as this. One day when I stand before Him to give an account of my life, this is all that will matter. The question is, "What kind of fruit can I offer to Him?"

The fruit that the Father desires is that which develops naturally as the result of a relationship. Not forced, and you do not have to struggle to produce it. As you abide in Christ, it just develops naturally.

He is not interested in the works of our flesh, which we are so often seeking to offer Him. Our works have no real value in the eyes of the Father. All our righteous works are as filthy rags in His sight. We must realize that it is the life of Christ flowing through us that produces the kind of fruit the Father desires. If you do not abide in Christ, you are cast forth as a branch and become withered.

If the branch does not bear fruit, it is taken away. There is nothing more worthless than a branch that does not bear fruit. Jesus spoke of the tree that did not bear fruit that the husbandman ordered it to be cut down. God spoke of all that He did for His vineyard that he might enjoy the fruit, and all it brought forth was wild grapes. God spoke of His judgment that would come upon that vineyard.

Those branches that bear fruit are purged that they may bring forth more fruit. "Now, you are clean through the word that I have spoken unto you." It is the Father's good will that you bring forth much fruit, so the next step in the process is abiding in Christ, and the result is that you will bear much fruit.

We desire that our lives produce lasting fruit. "Ye have not chosen me, but I have chosen you, and ordained you, that ye should go and bring forth fruit, and [that] your fruit should remain" (John 15:16). Jesus declares that the purpose of choosing us is not that we bring forth fruit. But that the fruit might remain. That is lasting fruit.

As believers of the Word, you need to see yourself as continually sowing seed in the fertile hearts of God's children. The seed is the Word of God, planting God's Word in their hearts. God said that His Word will not return unto Him void but will accomplish the purposes for which it was sent forth.

It is the Word of God that will bring lasting fruit. I pray that your life might bear fruit for our Lord. I pray that as you begin to bear fruit, you will bring forth more fruit. I pray that you might bring forth much fruit to the glory of God. I pray that the fruit might remain. The key is abiding in Him and His Word through the power of the Holy Spirit.

"I AM ALPHA AND OMEGA"

John adds yet one more "I Am," of a sort, in the Book of Revelation.

"I am the Alpha and the Omega," says the Lord God, "who is and who was and who is to come, the Almighty" (Revelation 1:8).

Writing about seeing Jesus, he shares, "I fell at his feet as though dead. But he laid his right hand on me, saying, "Fear not, I am the first and the last, and the living one. I died, and behold I am alive forevermore, and I have the keys of Death and Hades" (Revelation 1:17).

Now whether this is Jesus or God, it is immaterial. Because Jesus addresses John in a moment in verse eleven saying "I am the Alpha and Omega, the first and the last, and what you see write in a book." Now, if God declares of Himself that I am the Alpha and the Omega, the beginning and the ending, and Jesus states that I am the Alpha and the Omega, the beginning and the ending, then I AM that I AM is speaking, making them the same.

"In the beginning was the Word, and the Word was with God, and the Word was God. The same was in the beginning with God. All things were made by him; and without him was not anything made that was made" (John 1:1-3).

"And the Word was made flesh, and dwelt among us, (and we beheld his glory, the glory as of the only begotten of the Father,) full of grace and truth" (John 1:14).

A PROMISE

"Behold, I stand at the door, and knock: if any man hears my voice, and open the door, I will come into him, and will sup with him, and he with me. To him that overcometh will I grant to sit with me in my throne, even as I also overcame, and am set down with my Father in his throne. He that hath an ear, let him hear what the Spirit saith unto the churches" (Revelation 3:20-22).

THE "BORN AGAIN" PRAYER

If you don't know Jesus Christ as your personal Lord and Savior, you can receive Him into your heart by faith today. To receive Jesus as your personal Lord and Savior, pray this simple prayer:

"Father in Heaven, I believe you sent your Son, Jesus, from heaven; I believe He died for my sins on the Cross; I believe He rose on the third day and sits with you in heaven even now.

Please forgive me for my sins. Jesus, please come into my life as my Lord and Savior and guide me with Your Holy Spirit. Thank you, Father." In Jesus' name, I pray, AMEN!

"Welcome to God's kingdom, and may we fellowship throughout eternity."

2

BROKEN PROMISES

"A wholesome tongue is a tree of life: but perverseness therein is a breach in the spirit" (Proverbs 15:4).

Have you ever made a promise you didn't keep? If you are human, I'm sure the answer is YES. We might have good intentions when first conceived. New Year Resolutions are a great example of broken promises. Every year we promise ourselves and others to stop, give up, commit to, or just-plain change our ways.

There are many forms of guarantees we make. Some are honorable, misguided, or outright deceptive. If personal gain at the cost of others is the purpose of your promise, you should search your heart.

God is the Promise Maker and the Keeper of His Promises. Making promises to God is never a good use of our relationship with Him. For example, we tell God we can help Him catch two birds with one net. "God, if you let me date this beautiful non-believer, I promise to bring him/her to salvation! Just let me have my way, and you will gain another soul for your kingdom." God doesn't play that game!

For God tells us, "Do not be unequally yoked together with unbelievers" (2 Corinthians 6:14). You will be the one converted and not them. You can turn on the light but can't always turn off the darkness. I know this to be true because I played this game with God once, and He finally removed the temptation by relocating her to a different state.

A FISHER OF MEN

I have wonderful memories of camping with my dad and fishing at our favorite lakes and rivers. One sunny day we were walking down the trail with my new fishing pole straddling my shoulder, thinking how great of a dad I had. Suddenly, to my fearful surprise, I heard behind me, the screams and nasty words of my dad as if I had done something wrong. I turned around to inquire about all the noise. Never seeing my dad, just hearing his angry voice following behind me as I turned around and around and around. Finally, my dad's firm hand grabbed my shoulder and yelled out, "STOP MOVING!"

To my shock, I had caught a WHOPPER, and it was my dad. My fishing line had hooked him through the nose, and he was MAD! With his nose bleeding, me crying, the ride home was way too long. He told me he would never take me fishing again! I promised him I was sorry that I would be a good Son, and I would never disappoint him again. I was devastated that my dad would have that kind of reaction to an accident.

It took some time before we went fishing again. A happy camper and world-class fishing kid, pleasing my dad in every way. However, looking back over my life, there were hundreds of promises made and broken to my family and friends. I was a complete disappointment to my parents. My mom taught me how to wave goodbye to the ice-cream truck as it drove past our house. My dad helped me to lay-low when the Federal Marshals came knocking at his door.

Dysfunctional doesn't come close to the destructive dynamics I created in our family! My parents grew to dislike me. However, I later found a Heavenly Father who wanted all of me.

A WHOPPER BY ANY OTHER NAME

Confident the WHOPPER I caught as a child was not the kind of fish Jesus spoke about in Matthew 4:19-20, Then He said to them, "Follow Me, and I will make you fishers of men." They left their nets and followed Him.

The hook that caught my dad, which brought pain, is now a metaphor for my Calling in Christ. To follow Him, to be a Fisher of Men, I needed to leave my Nets behind. My Nets were my drugs, my sins, my old life, unkept promises, and lack of commitment to God's Divine Purpose.

I am to bait my hook with God's Truth and cast the line of Salvation out in the Name of Christ. I am to rely on the Holy Spirit to catch one person at a time for the Glory of God and His Eternal Plan. Discerning, we are all members of the Body of Christ with distinct functions and gifts. "Some plant, some water, but it's God that gives the increase…," (1 Corinthians 3:6).

God has called us to forsake all, pick up our Cross, follow him, and become fishers of men for the Gospel of Eternal Life in Christ. God was faithful in this part of my story because it ends well. When I stopped making promises to God, I received the ones He wanted to give me. Finally, allowing God to work in my life, He did make me a fisher of men. My parents experienced my transformation as I brought Glory to God. I lived and applied Matthew 5:16 before their eyes, "Let your light so shine before men, that they may see your good works, and glorify your Father which is in heaven."

Both parents allowed me to pray with them in their last days in the hospital. We all now have Eternity to love each other as God loves us. This story is a cautionary tale because God was telling me to share His Gospel, and I felt unworthy because of my past with them. Sometimes we feel like hypocrites.

Deciding to obey God, I went into my dad's room, expecting rejection. To my surprise, he was so excited that I prayed with him, and he committed his life to Jesus. We never know the day or the hour when we are to leave this world. My dad died within a few hours after our prayer. When the Spirit leads, we must take immediate advantage of God's appointed time. Had I waited another day for the courage to obey God, my dad would have died separated for all Eternity from our Lord.

A few years later, I visited my mom in the hospital and said, "Can we talk?" she excitedly said, "I was wondering when it was my turn." She was waiting to believe it! Amazingly, many people are just waiting for us to share Christ with them. Don't let past relationships or pride stop the conversation. God promises to use us for His glory and the benefit of His Church.

A lesson learned over and over is that; some plant, some water, but it is God that gives the increase. We are to testify of the salvation in Christ and let the Holy Spirit draw them to God. We cannot save anyone no matter what our motive is, good or bad. Until a person is ready, no amount of argument or desire from us will convince them we are right. We cannot push anyone into the kingdom. Only the conviction and drawing of the Holy Spirit will achieve this.

WAVERING FAITH UPON THE SEA

Throughout the Gospels, we learned many lessons concerning the Apostles of Christ. In particular, the stories of Peter are fascinating and are teachable moments for sure. He was the MOST IMPULSIVE Disciple, quick to speak, and slow to hear. He has gotten a bad rap from many people for his behavior.

However, he was the only disciple who got out of the boat when Jesus came walking on the seas. Even in the heights of Peter's triumphs, there was always a fall awaiting him around the next corner or verse.

Peter always has his spiritual highs, followed by a test of his faith. When he got out of the boat to see Jesus, his faith was strong. However, he didn't keep his eyes on Jesus and stumbled on the water. Therefore, Jesus states, "O thou of little faith."

"And Peter answered him and said, Lord, if it is, thou, bid me come unto thee on the water. And he said, Come. And when Peter was come down out of the ship, he walked on water to go to Jesus. But when he saw the wind boisterous, he was afraid; and beginning to sink, he cried, saying, Lord, save me. And immediately, Jesus stretched forth his hand, and caught him, and said unto him, O thou of little faith, wherefore didst thou doubt?" (Matthew 14: 28-31).

A great question to ponder is, "When does Jesus save us?" Let me help you out with this, "Whenever we cry out to Him." Lord, save me. And immediately, Jesus stretched forth his hand…"

Peter's problem was that he didn't keep his eyes on Jesus, the author, and finisher of his faith. Lack of focus is robbing us of genuinely following Christ throughout our lives. We miss the promises because our spiritual eyes are blind. We see ourselves in Peter all the time. Each time he had a spiritual revelation, a carnal decision followed.

The reason we see Peter as a failure is that we see ourselves in him. It's like we complain about so and so gossiping about someone as we continue to talk about that person. Are we sharing our thoughts and feelings, or are we gossipers? The things we see in others that bother us are usually the things within our lives needing fixing.

It's like the saying goes, "When you point your finger at others, three fingers are pointing back at you." We should first clean our house before we try to do spring cleaning in someone else's home. You without sin cast the first stone.

JESUS IS DEAD SERIOUS ABOUT HIS WORD

God's Word is much to do about everything. In fact, "Heaven and earth shall pass away, but my words shall not pass away" (Matthew 24:35). The BIBLE was written over 1,600 years, by 40 different authors, on three continents, in 3 languages, on 100's of subjects, with COMPLETE HARMONY, without CONTRADICTION! The SCRIPTURES have One Central Storyline, GOD'S REDEMPTION OF MANKIND THROUGH JESUS CHRIST (HIS SON) THE WORD OF GOD.

Absolute belief in God's Word is mandatory for every believer. Jesus is dead serious about His Word; in fact, He died to keep His Word. We so often try to assemble something without the owner's manual. God, in His divine wisdom, has supplied us instructions within the pages of scripture. Who better to teach us than the author and finisher of our faith (Jesus) in all doctrinal truths?

Believing our Lord has a divine purpose behind every promise will help us to respond based upon scriptural truth and not our feelings. With every Promise brings opportunities and responsibilities. God is more concerned about our character than our comfort. His goal is not to pamper us physically but to perfect us spiritually.

Jesus Christ declared, "I have come. In the volume of the book, it is written of Me." Therefore, Scripture should always be at the threshold of every decision we face. For it is God's Mind Written Down. It's like Jesus reciting Himself.

"HE WHO HAS EARS TO HEAR, LET HIM HEAR!"

When Jesus finished telling His parable of the Sower, He cried out: "He who has ears to hear, let him hear!" – (Matthew 13:9). Clearly, from the explanation of Jesus Himself, we learn that not all those who have ears to hear, really listen!

It's vital we actively listen to the spoken Word of God, for this is how we obtain faith. Romans 10:17, "So then faith comes by hearing and hearing by the word of God." A person cannot believe unless they hear. It is through the revelation of Scripture that we come to know Him. Thus, by knowing God, we come to believe and trust in Him.

The Word of God is essential for the development of faith within our hearts, minds, and lives.

The Book of Hebrews is a treasure trove of blessings for us. Its writer proclaims, "Now faith is the substance of things hoped for, the evidence of things not seen" (Hebrew 11:1). A declaration of what faith does, and the things hoped for is its substance.

Hope is unseen; it is yet future, such as hoping for eternal life or even the end of a trial. Our faith is in Jesus, and He is the substance (everything which goes into making our faith possible, as well as our reason for belief and the answer to everything). And He is all the things we hope for, (eternal life, deliverance, promises, new bodies, experience, rewards, etc.), which makes him the evidence of the things not seen.

There is evidence for the existence of God, and it causes us to believe in Him. Though we have never seen God, the proof of His life creates that measure of faith in our hearts that all things are possible and real when God's Word says so. Knowing that (God is for us, God is with us, and God is in us) gives us hope, faith, and evidence that the substance is God Himself! Our spirit bears witness that our faith is the assurance of things hoped for, the proving of things not seen.

FAITH IS OUR LIFELINE TO GOD

We obtain salvation by faith; we walk in faith; we live by faith; we bring glory to God when we grow in faith, and someday, we will receive rewards because of our faith. Ask God to increase your confidence and show you how to apply it in everything you do because we must have it to serve our Lord.

Hebrews 11:6 states, "But without faith, it is impossible to please Him, for he who comes to God must believe that He is and that He is a rewarder of those who diligently seek Him." It is interesting to note this scripture points out that we first do the will of God, and then with patience, we wait to receive the promise. So, in faith, we do the will of God by believing He will perform, then with patience, we await the sign of His working, which is our hope. It is through our endurance and its fruit-bearing that makes alive our soul, our new life unto God.

Our souls live and have substance through our patience, for through our patience, we are spiritually alive in Christ and await the promise of eternal life, which flesh, and blood cannot inherit. Therefore, we believe that God is good and rewards those who diligently seek Him.

Faith is the gift from God that allows us to trust in all His promises. Our belief is the revelation of Scripture. The substance of faith believes in what isn't visible and what isn't perceived or experienced.

What we hope for by way of revealed promises has substance right now, also being the assurance of all God's promises made about our future. All because we believe in the truth of God's revelation in His revealed Scripture. We have hope so strong that it can change our lives, and this reality gives weight to our purpose in life.

This faith is so powerful it trains the heart to believe the revealed promises of God and is an anchor laid out in the experiences of believers. Real faith gives us a specific substance in the present, which fortifies our future hope.

It's not just the assurance or substance or evidence, but it's also the conviction of things not seen. It is the substance that becomes a conviction, and it's the conviction that defines how you live. You can know that something is right, but until it becomes a conviction, you do not put it into action. So, we have a substance that has become our conviction, which leads to strong faith and righteous living.

STRONG FAITH AND A LARGE BOAT

What would make you build a boat in the middle of the desert when it had never rained in the history of the world? Would it be a conviction? It would have to be something more than hope because you must spend 120 years building the boat. For sure, Noah dealt with the mockery of his neighbors, but he persevered in fulfilling God's will.

The book of Hebrews is known as the 'Hall of Faith' because the writer points out how faith was the way the

Saints of old gained approval. They lived their lives based on the promises God gave to them. God's Word made their hope real, turning their faith into a confident trust in the future promised by God in Scripture.

Concluding this thought: When going through a trial, seeking a promise, the substance of things hoped for is God providing for all our needs. He works on us and guides us through the test, and it becomes the visible evidence of things once not seen. Giving us hope when the next trial comes because of the evidence of His workings. Thus, God is the substance, hope, and proof that He is working through our faith and trials.

INCREASE YOUR MEASURE OF FAITH

God has given every man a measure of faith. The faith that we have in our heart is a gift of God. Paul said, "By grace are you saved through faith, and that not of yourself; it's a gift of God. Not of works lest any man should boast" (Ephesians 2:8). Our salvation, the faith by which we believe, is God's gift. In I Corinthians 12, Paul lists faith as one of the gifts of the Spirit.

Scripture portrays the Christian life as a walk. It speaks of walking in the Spirit, walking in the flesh, walking in Light, walking in Darkness, walking in love, and walking in the truth. The Lord made a bold statement about faith, "Jesus answered and said unto them, Verily I say unto you, If ye have faith, and doubt not, ye shall not only do this which is done to the fig tree, but also if ye shall say unto this mountain, Be thou removed, and be thou cast into the sea; it shall be done. And all things, whatsoever ye shall ask in prayer, believing, ye shall receive" (Matthew 21:21-22).

Knowing and believing what the Word says about itself and the promises therein, will help your walk with God and the fiery trials coming your way. Let the author of the Word teach you in all things about life. Knowing the truth will set you free.

THE ROADMAP FOR GOD'S WORD

The Good News is we have a roadmap to follow, and it is the WORD of GOD. If we lack understanding, ask God in prayer, and He will increase our faith to understand His wisdom and truth.

Following is an excellent roadmap to guide us and equip us to apply His Word as we move toward eternity. Keeping our eyes upon the prize that is in Christ Jesus, let's commit ourselves to the leading and inspiration of the Holy Spirit. The Word will lead you, instruct you, mature you, protect you, and supply promises needed to escape the fiery trials of life.

Knowledge is the Apprehension of TRUTH in one's mind, but Wisdom is the Application of TRUTH to one's life.

"But be ye doers of the word, and not hearers only, deceiving yourselves" (James 1:22).

THE GOAL OF THE WORD: To "study to shew thyself approved unto God, a workman that needeth not to be ashamed, rightly dividing the word of truth" (2 Timothy 2:15).

THE PURPOSE OF THE WORD: "All scripture is given by inspiration of God, and is profitable for doctrine, for reproof, for correction, for instruction in righteousness: That the man of God may be perfect, thoroughly furnished unto all good works" (2 Timothy 3:16-17).

THE QUESTIONS CONCERNING THE WORD:

- Are there any Examples for me to Follow?
- Are there any Commands for me to Obey?
- Are there any Errors for me to Avoid?
- Are there any SINS for me to Forsake?
- Are there any New Thoughts about GOD Himself?
- Are there any Promises for me to Apply?
- Are there any Principles I must Accept?

THE PROMISE FROM THE WORD: "But the Comforter, which is the Holy Ghost, whom the Father will send in my name, he shall teach you all things, and bring all things to your remembrance, whatsoever I have said unto you" (John 14:26).

"Thy WORD is a Lamp unto my Feet and a Light unto my Path"

(Psalm 119: 105).

Jesus is the Word & God is the Promises Keeper

https://thewordisjesus.com/

PROMISES

Salvation is summed up by Paul in Romans, "That if thou shalt confess with thy mouth the Lord Jesus, and shalt believe in thine heart that God hath raised him from the dead, thou shalt be saved. For with the heart, man believeth unto righteousness; and with the mouth, confession is made unto salvation" (Romans 10:9-10).

"Being confident of this very thing, that he which hath begun a good work in you will perform it until the day of Jesus Christ" (Philippians 1:6).

A PRAYER

Dear Lord, I am grateful that You have made a way for me to move from death to life. Remind me that this is a gift of Your grace, and not a result of anything I have done, or can do. Keep me aware that the "old man" in me will always look to draw me back to that way of death. May I trust and apply the Word in everything about life. Teach me eternal lessons to share with others. I pray these things in the gracious name of Jesus, AMEN.

3

LIAR-LIAR, PANTS ON FIRE

"But above all, my brethren, do not swear, either by heaven or by earth or with any other oath. But let your "Yes" be "Yes," and your "No," "No," lest you fall into judgment."
(James 5:12)

When I was young, we played many games. If you were caught in a lie or cheating, we would yell out, "Liar-Liar, Pants on Fire, Nose as Long as a Telephone wire!" The Castaways recorded Liar-Liar – in 1965. When I think about the global depravity, this song should be the New World Order Anthem.

People today never lie; they miss-remembered or miss-spoked. Never an apology or a correction to the record. With the damage done, lives ruined, the news cycle marches on.

Promises are to be kept or not made at all. In Matthew Chapter 26, we find one of the most significant broken promises in all the Bible. Peter promised Jesus that he would never stumble or never deny Him. Jesus said to him, "Assuredly, I say to you that this night before the rooster crows, you will deny Me three times." Peter did deny Him three times as Jesus foretold. And Peter remembered the word of Jesus who had said to him, "Before the rooster crows, you will deny Me three times." So, he went out and wept bitterly."

Our promises should be commitments to God made in faith, founded in His Word, approved by His will, implemented through His principles, for the improvement of the Church and bringing Glory to God. Our eternal relationship is more significant than our gratification. God is more concerned with our character than our comfort. His goal is not to pamper us physically but to perfect us spiritually.

When you think about it, these lessons we learn through Peters spiritual highs and carnal lows represent our Christian walk. We confess Christ as Lord, then as we sojourn, we deny Him, we backslide, we have seasons of the soul and we must repent. God is gracious to restore us when we ask Him for forgiveness. Peter in one breath proclaimed Jesus to be the Messiah, the Son of the living God. Next breath we find him rebuking Jesus.

WHO AM I TO YOU?

Jesus asked the Disciples, "Who do men say I am?" Simon Peter answered and said, "You are the Christ, the Son of the living God." "Jesus answered and said to him, "Blessed are you, Simon Bar-Jonah, for flesh and blood has not revealed this to you, but My Father who is in heaven. That thou art Peter, and upon this rock, I will build my church; and the gates of hell shall not prevail against it."

In Jesus' day, there were many stories as to who He was, with some saying John the Baptist, others suggesting Elijah, Jeremiah, or some other prophet. But the crucial question Jesus asked his disciples was, "But who do you say that I am?"

Peter was commended for his great answer, "You are the Christ, the Son of the living God." He recognized Jesus as the Messiah (the anointed One) and as the Son of God (making him equal with God).

The most important question you will ever have to answer in your life is the same question: Who is Jesus? Your eternity hangs on the answer to that simple question.

A SPIRITUAL VICTORY ROBBED BY CARNAL THOUGHTS

Jesus began to show to His disciples that He must go to Jerusalem and suffer many things from the elders and chief priests. They would kill Him, but He would rise on the third day.

Then Peter took Him aside and began to rebuke Him, saying, "Far be it from You, Lord; this shall not happen to You!" But He turned and said to Peter, "Get behind Me, Satan! You are an offense to Me, for you are not mindful of the things of God, but the things of men."

So, Peter has a divine revelation, then comes the inspiration of his own heart inspired by Satan. Such a common problem with us, the ability to know the difference between when God is speaking and when my own heart is speaking to me.

This spiritual victory is annulled by allowing his flesh to rob and rule the moment. In one breath he has a divine revelation, and in the next, is expressing Satan's philosophy. Spare yourself. "Be that far from thee," literally, spare thyself; it shall not be to you. This was one of the devil's temptations he tried on Jesus in the wilderness.

The worlds philosophy lies to us saying, "Take the easy path and escape the cross." So often encouraged by this fallen world to use the Short Cut Lie, to avoid the cross. But the cross was essential for our Salvation. Thus, picking it up daily and denying ourselves is vital to our spiritual development.

The path of discipleship is the path of self-denial, the way of the cross. I must come to the cross in my own life. I must come to the end of my ambitions, my personal goals, my desires, and reckon that old life of the flesh to be dead, crucified with Christ, that I might live a new life after the Spirit in Christ Jesus.

We are called to preach the gospel for the glory of God and the benefit of the unsaved. And to teach the Word for the edification of the body of Christ. Thus, our calling is confirmed as we do what we are commanded to do in Christ.

Confess Christ as Lord unto salvation. Love Him more than life itself. Leave your old life behind, pick up your cross and follow Him into eternity.

WILL YOU LAY DOWN YOUR LIFE FOR MY SAKE?

Jesus said all of you are going to be offended tonight because of me. Peter said, "Lord, though they may offend you, I will never be offended." Boasting in the flesh. I will never be offended. In a sense, he is declaring that his love was superior to the love of the other disciples.

Simon Peter said to Him, "Lord, where are You going?" Jesus answered him, "Where I am going, you cannot follow Me now, but you shall follow Me afterward." Peter said to Him, "Lord, why can I not follow You now? I will lay down my life for Your sake."

Jesus answered him, "Will you lay down your life for My sake? Most assuredly, I say to you; the rooster shall not crow till you have denied Me three times. And he did.

FISHERS OF MEN NO LONGER CATCH WHOPPERS

Picking up on our story after the resurrection. "Now this is the third time that Jesus showed himself to the disciples after he rose from the dead. So, when they had eaten breakfast, Jesus said to Simon Peter, "Simon, son of Jonah, do you love Me more than these?" He said to Him, "Yes, Lord; You know that I love You." He said to him, "Feed My lambs."

Peter had denied Christ three times, and Jesus restores him with three questions followed by three commands. If you love me feed my sheep. God always allows us to reflect and repent.

Exhorting them to get with the program He says, "You're not to be out here fishing. I told you to leave your nets and to follow Me. I'll make you fishers of men. Now, feed My lambs." The Lord is interested that His lambs are fed. Jeremiah said that "The Lord will give them in that day pastors after His own heart, who will feed them with knowledge and understanding." That would be the knowledge and understanding of God.

The first time Peter was asked "do you love me?"; Jesus uses the word agape for love. This word was the word in

Greek that the New Testament writers used to represent a supreme, sacrificial love. Peter responded by saying that he was fond of Jesus.

He used the word for love that is in the Greek phileo. It usually denotes a brotherly love. The third time Jesus used the word phileo as He asked Peter if he loved Him. Peter was grieved and he eventually responded that he had phileo love for Jesus. Peter never rose to the level of agape love for Jesus until after the Day of Pentecost.

He said to him again a second time, "Simon, son of Jonah,] do you love Me?" He said to Him, "Yes, Lord; You know that I love You." He said to him, "Tend My sheep."

He said to him the third time, "Simon, son of Jonah, do you love Me?" Peter grieved because He said to him the third time, "Do you love Me?" And he said to Him, "Lord, you know all things; You know that I love You." Jesus said to him, "Feed My sheep."

This time, Jesus used Peter's word, phileo. "Peter, are you fond of Me?" And Peter was grieved because this third time, Jesus used Peter's terms and said, "Are you fond of Me?" It hurt Peter deeply that Jesus had reduced Himself to Peter's level.

God will always meet us on whatever level we will meet Him. But it is tragic when we bring God down to our level, rather than rising to His standards. However, God will meet us on whatever level we will meet Him. It is tragic that we limit God in our lives because we won't rise to the degree that God desires. Can you count on one hand how many promises you've missed while seeking your own standards? Can you count to infinity?

"IF YOU LOVE ME MORE THAN THESE, FEED MY SHEEP"

What is this love Jesus is asking of? It is supreme love. It is giving love, a divine, intense, more than worldly kinds of love.

What were the "these"? Maybe the one hundred fifty-three fish still flopping in the nets over there. "Do you love Me more than your livelihood? Do you love Me more than the greatest success in your chosen profession? Having the height of success in your chosen field, do you love Me more than that, Peter? How much do you love Me? Do you love Me more than these?"

What are these, those, and this in your life, interfering with God's purpose? Jesus asked Peter if he loved Him supremely. The disciples had just had the most significant day in their lives as fishermen. The fish were flopping all over the place, and this represented professional success to Peter. But Jesus wanted to know if he loved Him more than professional success.

Our Lord would ask each of us the same questions. "What priority am I in your life?" "How far down am I on the list of things you care about?" And I believe He would ask each of us, "How much do you love Me?" "How many things in your life are more important to you then I am?" Tough question, but it is an important question.

To serve Jesus, you need to love Him more than anything else. "These" represents something different to each of us, but we need to ask ourselves if there is anything in our lives more important than our relationship with Jesus.

THE PRICE OF A SOUL

Is your soul on the Auction block? What will a man give in exchange for his soul? Now, as far as God is concerned, your soul is worth more than the whole world. If you were offered the world in trade for your soul and exchanged it, you'd be making a bad deal, a stupid deal. Your soul is eternal.

The world is going to pass away and the lust thereof. Then the question, "what will a man give in exchange for his soul?" What would you take for your soul? Some of you, who have been wandering in the wilderness in your Christian experience, maintaining a barren soul, God is calling you to pass over Jordan, and come into the promised land.

Enter the land of milk and honey He has promised, where the life of the Spirit lives in victory through the power of the Holy Spirit. Give your soul to God, give Him your life in those areas where your flesh has kept you in defeat before.

A PROMISE
"I AM THE WAY, THE TRUTH, AND THE LIFE"

"He that hath an ear, let him hear what the Spirit saith unto the churches; To him that overcometh will I give to eat of the tree of life, which is in the midst of the paradise of God" (Revelation 2:7).

A PRAYER

God, this world's problems are so complicated that I cannot make my way without your guidance. Quicken my mind and deepen my understanding. Help me hear your voice and heed your advice. Keep me walking along the path behind you. Let me know your truth and set me free in thee. In Jesus' name - Amen.

4

I AM THE PROMISE-KEEPER

"For all the promises of God in Him are Yes, and in Him Amen, to the glory of God through us" (2 Corinthians 1:20).

GOD FULFILLS HIS PROMISES

"God's promises will expire (in the twinkling of an eye) between our last breath and our entrance into eternity."

In human terms, promises are easily broken. In God's terms, they are a sure thing. Knowing what God has promised us and how he keeps his promises gives us assurance, hope, and peace.

God has made many promises that He intends to keep. However, they are not without action on our part. Designed to bless us, assuming we meet His conditions. Those seeking to utilize any guarantee should be Seeking

Him, Walking with Him, Living in Him, and Obeying Him.

There are over 3,000 promises in the Bible and finding one for any need is possible with God's guidance. However, we must believe in faith that God will fulfill His promises. Then we apply the principles of scripture to receive the benefits of His blessings. It is not enough to read a pledge, name it and claim it, expecting God to apply it in your life. Nor is it God's "Blab It and Grab It Doctrine"! God doesn't play that game!

With every Promise comes Principles, we as Believers must apply, or they don't work. For unbelievers, the promises they should be seeking are the ones leading to salvation. <u>John 3:16 will bless them eternally</u>.

A PARAPHRASED EXAMPLE OF THE PROMISE IN JOHN 3:16

"For God so loved the world, that he gave his only begotten Son, that whosoever believeth in him should not perish, but have everlasting life."

God's past promises meet our present response. Given freely, we in faith, accept and apply them to our lives. Faith is believing God's Word and acting upon it.

Put another way, God is saying "If you do this, I will do that, because I have already done this." Thus, God's past promises meet our prompt response. His predetermined plan for us included His Promises.

Therefore, we have a past promise (working) that if we in faith believe in Jesus Christ and are born again, we will receive eternal life. We must apply this promise through the principle of faith. Without God's principles, the process of transforming us into the image of Christ will not take root to change our lives.

- THE PROMISE - Everlasting Life
- THE PERSON – Jesus, God's Only Begotten Son
- THE PURPOSE – Never Condemned
- THE PRINCIPLE – Believe What God Has Said
- THE PROCESS - The Cross of Christ

JESUS' past workings (on the Cross) meets our believing God's Word (confession of sins) producing (salvation and redemption) with our prompt response. Accepting and applying promises will save us, change us, heal us, conform us, and prepare us to exhort and comfort others.

The reason God can keep promises is that He made them and created the path to their fulfillment. God says, if you faithfully believe and apply them, I will fulfill them because I've already prepaid and prepared the way beforehand.

GOD WILL MOVE HEAVEN AND EARTH TO BLESS YOU

God's omnipotent power behind His Promises and Principles cannot be stopped by human force. Nothing on this earth or in the universe, whether visible or invisible, can prevent what God has promised for those who are His children. His promises are sure and true. If God wants to bless you, nothing will hinder His Promise. "What then shall we say to these things? If God is for us, who can be against us?" (Romans 8:31).

We can trust in them, lean upon them, apply them, and have the assurance that what God promises, He delivers through His effectual power to bring to pass all that His Word proclaims. It was by His Word that the universe came into existence, "For he spoke, and it came to be; he commanded, and it stood firm" (Psalm 33:9), and "we understand that the universe was created by the Word of God" (Hebrews 11:3).

A promise is only as reliable as the one who makes it. When God makes a promise, He will keep it, and you can believe it to be true.

Numbers 23:19 states, "God is not a man, that He should lie, nor a son of man, that He should repent. Has He said, and will He not do? Or has He spoken, and will He not make it good?"

Because some circumstances are beyond our control, we can't always keep our promises, but the Sovereign Lord of the Universe has never failed to fulfill His Word.

To understand how important the Lord's faithfulness is, we must recognize that the Christian life is dependent upon His promises. For example, the only reason we're certain we have Eternal Life, a home in heaven, and resurrected bodies awaiting us, is because Jesus guaranteed these things to His followers. The Bible is full of God's promises, but the most important thing to remember is not how many there are, but the fact that He keeps every single one. We must understand just how able and powerful He is.

We first believe in faith that God will fulfill His promise, and then we apply the Principles of teaching by doing those things that prove we accept and love God. You say you have faith then prove it.

James urges us to practice what we preach, "But be doers of the word, and not hearers only, deceiving yourselves. For if anyone is a hearer of the word and not a doer, he is like a man observing his natural face in a mirror; for he observes himself, goes away, and immediately forgets what kind of man he was" (James 1:22-24).

"I AM GOD ALMIGHTY"

I AM - Omniscient (Hebrews 4:13)—God knows every detail of a situation. From His perspective, He can see all our lives from beginning to end. Every promise He makes is based on His infinite, perfect, and complete knowledge, which means He never makes a mistake.

> I AM - Omnipresent (Hebrews 13:5)—No matter what we're going through, He will never leave nor forsake us. His continual presence guarantees the fulfillment of every promise.
>
> I AM - Omnipotent (Psalms 103:19)—Because the Lord is entirely sovereign over heaven and earth, nothing is out of His control. He has absolute power and authority, and nothing is too complicated for Him. (Jeremiah 32:17)

A promise is a verbal or written commitment to perform a specific act or to refrain from doing something. Therefore, a divine oath is God's assurance that He will do what He says. You can bet your life on it!

BEHIND EVERY PROMISE LIES A PRINCIPLE

God has promised many glorious things for those living by faith in His Son, our Eternal Redeemer. God's great love has provided us a way to reunite with Him and live the life he planned for us from the beginning. The Promise to send His Son to die on the cross for us has Principles and Processes we must apply.

God's past promises meet our present response. And, "Faith is believing God's Word and acting upon it." If the Promise is Eternal Life through His Son, then the Principle of believing in faith becomes the Process leading to our Born-Again experience. With every Promise, there are Principles we must follow, which become the Processes for application.

All His commandments, rules, and advice are founded upon Promises and Principles, given to us for our protection. Violating any of God's commandments or His advice violates His Principles of life! So, God's Processes are the glue that holds together His Promises and Principles. Thus, producing His perfect will and purpose in our lives.

Every promise comes with conditions, we as believers must apply, or they don't work. To emphasize, God is saying, "if you do this, I will do that because I have already done this." Thus, His preordained plan for us included His Promises.

PROMISES

"For all the promises of God in him are yea, and in him Amen, unto the glory of God by us. Now he which established us with you in Christ, and hath anointed us, is God; Who hath also sealed us, and given the earnest of the Spirit in our hearts" (1 Corinthians 1:20-22).

"So, shall my word be that goeth forth out of my mouth: it shall not return unto me void, but it shall accomplish that which I please, and it shall prosper in the thing whereto I sent it" (Isaiah 55:11).

"Wherein God, willing more abundantly to shew unto the heirs of promise the immutability of his counsel, confirmed it by an oath: That by two immutable things, in which it was impossible for God to lie, we might have a strong consolation, who have fled for refuge to lay hold upon the hope set before us" (Hebrews 6:17-18).

A PRAYER

Dear Father, thank you for being the promise keeper. May I receive in faith the promises you desire for my life. Might Your Purpose be achieved through me for your glory. Please increase my knowledge of Your Word and teach me how to apply the principles according to Your will. May I always obey your commands and seek you daily. Might I grow in faith and always be ready to share the gospel of salvation with ones you send my way. In Jesus' name, Amen and Amen.

5

DON'T CHERRY PICK THE TREE OF LIFE

"The fruit of the righteous is a tree of life; and he that wins souls is wise" (Proverbs 11:30).

APPLY WISDOM TO YOUR FREE CHOICE

Since we have free choice, we must make our decisions in life wisely. We need faith in God to begin anything we try to do. Applied wisdom is critical to the trials and temptations of life we face.

"Get wisdom, get understanding: forget it not; neither decline from the words of my mouth. Forsake her not, and she shall preserve thee: love her, and she shall keep thee. Wisdom is the principal thing; therefore, get wisdom: and with all thy getting get understanding" (Proverbs 4:5-7).

Temptation is familiar to us all. We will face it for the rest of our lives. There is no escape other than through Jesus. Spiritual maturity only causes Satan to increase pressure. The devil attacks us in all areas of our life, trying to deceive us and draw us away from our walk with God. Nevertheless, the Word of God helps us to overcome the things of this world.

<u>The devil tempts us in these three areas</u>:

1. Tempted to let our flesh dominate and rule over the Spirit. Sadly, we allow our flesh to get its way when we know in our spirit and soul, and that our actions would be displeasing to God.

2. He tempts us to test God by misusing His Word and by looking for loopholes to do what we want to do.

3. And finally, tempted to take shortcuts, to find ways of getting satisfaction and fulfillment without going the direction of the Cross and picking it up daily to follow Jesus. We need to resist Satan's lies with God's truth.

Understand, these lies are to tempt us to deny our Christ. But know that what comes out of the mouth of God is the number one priority in life. Speaking His TRUTH will protect our lives and bring glory to Him. Life should be about uninterrupted fellowship with God the Father, Jesus Christ the Son, and the Holy Spirit. Falling for lies, consumed by the things of this world, will not fulfill God's purpose for our lives.

God looks to draw us to obedience through love.

Satan seeks to entice us to disobey through lust.

THE DANGERS OF CHERRY-PICKING SCRIPTURE

Christians miss many Promises and blessings from God due to their carnal mindset. They don't go to church because all the people attending are hypocrites. As the saying goes, "If you find a perfect church, don't join it because it will no longer be perfect." Some Christians can't wait to get to heaven to validate their earthly concepts. God doesn't play that game.

If we have a position on various Scriptures that are not related to Doctrine, it will not interfere with our Salvation. For example, many debate the Rapture of the Church. When does Christ come for His Church? Pre-Tribulation, Mid-Tribulation, or Post-Tribulation. Our position doesn't matter in God's Plan of Salvation. God will take His Bride out in His time. It will happen when it happens; we only need to be ready. Not even Jesus knows the day or the hour.

Where it's right to hold an opinion, it is not right to let that opinion hold you. The pessimist sees the glass half empty, the optimist sees the glass half full, but the Psalmist proclaims, "My cup runneth over…" (Psalm 23:5) Our views on reality might be different from mind to mind, but our opinion doesn't give us a pass on eternal matters. We must still have our Salvation worked out before the coming of the Lord. Remember, there are no do-overs once we leave this world.

READ THE COMPLETE SCRIPTURE

Knowing, believing, and applying what the Word says will help our walk with God and the fiery trials coming our way. Knowing that the truth will set us free, we must rely on the author and finisher of our faith (Jesus) to teach us the doctrinal truth in everything. "All scripture is given by inspiration of God and is profitable for doctrine, for reproof, for correction, for instruction in righteousness: That the man of God may be perfect, thoroughly furnished unto all good works" (2 Timothy 3:16-17).

The most memorized, quoted, misused, and neglected verse in all the Bible is John 3:16. "For God so loved the world that He gave His only begotten Son, that whoever believes in Him should not perish but have everlasting life."

We are quick to bypass promises or to run with them, taking them out of context. In many cases, we neglect to read the complete Scripture, missing the consequences of not adhering to what God has conveyed. If we read past

John 3:16 to verse 19, we understand that God made a promise with implications for those not applying this life-saving promise.

Reading on, John 3:17-19, "For God did not send His Son into the world to condemn the world, but that the world through Him might be saved. He who believes in Him is not condemned, but he who does not believe is condemned already because he has not believed in the name of the only begotten Son of God. And this is the condemnation, that the light has come into the world, and men loved darkness rather than light because their deeds were evil."

Reading and understanding the full context of Scripture is the only way it applies to our lives. Although given freely, we need to perform our part to obtain the promise. Timothy points out one benefit of God's Word, "Study to shew thyself approved unto God, a workman that needeth not to be ashamed, rightly dividing the word of truth" (2 Timothy 2:15).

God has not given us His Word to hop-skip or jump around to see if something skips off the page at us that will support our preconceived ideas. This method will never satisfy God's desire for us in any situation.

If the only approach you take in discovering God's Will is opening the Bible and pointing your finger at a Scripture, you are deceiving yourself. Life consists of many decisions, combined with some skills. If you know the rules, the principles, and the strategies, you will be successful on earth, pleasing to God, performing His will and living throughout all eternity in heaven. AMEN and AMEN!

TO OBEY IS BETTER THAN SACRIFICE

Because the Lord is adequate and faithful, we have a perfect assurance that He will keep His promises. However, we must position ourselves to receive what He wants to provide.

"And Samuel said, Hath the LORD as great delight in burnt offerings and sacrifices, as in obeying the voice of the LORD? Behold, to obey is better than sacrifice, and to hearken than the fat of rams" (1 Samuel 15:22).

> OBEY GOD: Throughout the Old Testament, the Lord issued covenants conditioned upon obedience (Deuteronomy 28). If we've asked God for something and He hasn't yet provided it, we need to search our hearts to see if we've did not obey Him in some area. Did we miss the Principle? Maybe God wants us to wait, or we don't need it in God's Eternal Plan for us.

> BELIEVE THE LORD: Faith is an indispensable requirement. Always ask yourself if you sincerely trust Him to fulfill His Word. If you lack faith, ask God to

increase your confidence. Remember, you can improve your loyalty, "So then faith cometh by hearing, and hearing by the word of God" (Romans 10:17).

APPLY THE PROMISE: When we believe the Lord will do what He says, we can confidently receive and apply the promise for ourselves. But if we have doubts, feel concerned and worried even after praying about it, this will hinder our prayer requests.

Many people are close to receiving God's best, yet they can't get over the obstacle of unbelief. They know the Lord fulfilled promises in the past but doubt He will do the same for them. We should make it our goal to confidently say, "God said it, I believe it, and that settles it!" Then we'll have the confidence to live fruitful, abundant lives knowing that God is committed to doing what's best for us.

If We Can Completely Believe Some of God's Promises, Why Do We Have Difficulty Believing All?

So, what does the LORD require? "He hath shewed thee, O man, what is good; and what doth the LORD requires of thee, but to do justly, and to love mercy, and to walk humbly with thy God?" (Micha 6:18)

God is faithful – you can bet your life upon it!

A PROMISE

"And he shewed me a pure river of water of life, clear as crystal, proceeding out of the throne of God and of the Lamb.

In the midst of the street of it, and on either side of the river, was there the tree of life, which bare twelve manner of fruits, and yielded her fruit every month: and the leaves of the tree were for the healing of the nations.

And there shall be no more curse: but the throne of God and of the Lamb shall be in it; and his servants shall serve him:

And they shall see his face; and his name shall be in their foreheads.

And there shall be no night there; and they need no candle, neither light of the sun; for the Lord God giveth them light: and they shall reign for ever and ever.

And he said unto me, these sayings are faithful and true: and the Lord God of the holy prophets sent his angel to shew unto his servants the things which must shortly be done.

Behold, I come quickly: blessed is he that keepeth the sayings of the prophecy of this book" (Revelation 22:1-7).

A PRAYER

Dear God, help me to live a committed life sanctified through your holy scripture. Give me a burning desire to increase my faith and lean not to my own understanding. I acknowledge your path is the right road for me to travel. Give me wisdom in all decisions and let me drink of your living water. Help me bring my thoughts under control by putting on the mind of Christ. Utmost correct me and hear me when I cry out for forgiveness. In Jesus's name-AMEN

6

THE SHORT CUT LIE IS QUID PRO QUO

"Be sober, be vigilant; because your adversary the devil, as a roaring lion, walketh about, seeking whom he may devour" (1 Peter 5:8).

FALLING HARD IN THE GARDEN

GOD'S instruction to Adam and Eve was that they could eat any fruit in the Garden of Eden except one. He said: "But of the tree of the knowledge of good and evil, you shall not eat, for in the day that you eat of it you shall surely die" (Genesis 2:17).

We so often try to assemble something without the owner's manual. Likewise, we try to win a spiritual battle without the armor of God protecting us. Sadly, prayer becomes the final cry for God's help after first trying all carnal options and worsening the problem through our misguided self-determination!

God created everything in the Garden for Adam and Eve to eternally enjoy. However, He gave them one commandment to obey, and they failed by listening to the lies of the serpent. Paraphrased, "don't eat it, or you will die." The Word precisely says what God said!

Eve's main problem was that she had a conversation with Satan in the first place! Scripture states: "Submit yourselves therefore to God. Resist the devil, and he will flee from you. Draw nigh to God, and he will draw nigh to you" (James 4:7-8a).

Half-truths, lies, the world, and our old nature, which includes pride and greed are some of the most common strategies Satan uses to tempt us to sin against God. His goal is to keep us from God and eternal life. Reflecting the Image of God by the renewing of our minds is our calling now.

We win the battle for control over our mind as we 'put on the whole armor of God.' The helmet of salvation will serve us well as we move forward in our relationship with God. The Apostle Paul writes, "For the weapons of our warfare are not carnal, but mighty through God to the pulling down of strongholds; Casting down imaginations, and every high thing that exalteth itself against the knowledge of God and bring into captivity every thought to the obedience of Christ" (2 Corinthians 10:4-5).

THE TRUTH EQUATION: A changed life will always be the result of a renewed mind; a renewed spirit always results in a transformed life.

THE FAR-LEFT SIDE OF STUPID

"Therefore, if any man [be] in Christ, [he is] a new creature: old things are passed away; behold, all things are become new"

(2 Corinthians 5:17).

We need to get our minds under control. Putting on the mind of Christ is essential in controlling our thought life. But first, we must put off our old carnal mind. God has made promises and provisions for us to change our way of thinking. His Word instructs us on how to submit to the will of God. As we have discovered in earlier chapters, God's ways are not our ways.

When we start to think in a carnal way, we must stop our thoughts, take dominion over them in Jesus' name, and "not be conformed to this world, but be transformed by the renewing of your mind" (Romans 12:2). The question should always be, "What would Jesus think and do?"

Changing our perspective is vital in winning our spiritual battles. Scripture has commanded us to "Put on The Whole Armor of God." Once on, we are to keep it on. Our victory in spiritual battles come in the power of the Holy Spirit. We prepare for warfare by bringing our thoughts into captivity and obedience by asking yourself in all situations, "what would Jesus think, do, or say," and then imitate Him.

Although we walk in the flesh, that is, we are in a body of flesh; our real warfare is not fleshly. Paul, writing to the Ephesians, said, "For we wrestle not against flesh and blood, but against principalities, and powers, and spiritual entities in high places" (Ephesians 6:12).

"We walk in the weakness of the flesh," but though we WALK in it, we do not WAR according to it. We walk in faith and not by sight. Thus, the importance of increasing our confidence. Paul exhorts us concerning one piece of armor much needed, "above all, taking the shield of faith, wherewith ye shall be able to quench all the fiery darts of the wicked" (Ephesians 6:16).

Being destined to be like Him, He is the only "pattern" we must follow. And because He lives His life in us, we too can "walk even as He walked," "do as He did," "love as He loved," "forgive as He forgave," and "have this mind which was also in Christ Jesus."

GOD DOESN'T PLAY THAT GAME!

The vanity of humanity with their vain imaginations are the strongholds that bind up the hearts of men — crafting arguments against God, holding on to every high thing that exalts itself against the knowledge of God. We miss it entirely if we think the love of manipulation, the image of success, smooth words, the feeling of power, lording over authority, and human schemes and programs are just problems among unbelievers. Paul dealt with these types of hearts and minds in the church.

When we start to think in this carnal way, we must stop our thoughts, take dominion over them in Jesus' name. We can choose to prevent this kind of thinking by bringing every thought into captivity to the obedience of Christ. Deny feelings of lust, thoughts of anger, thoughts of fear, thoughts of greed, bitter ideas, and evil thoughts.

If you are a Christian, you are a purchased possession of Jesus Christ. You belong to Him. Paul puts it this way: "Or do you not know that your body is the temple of the Holy Spirit who is in you, whom you have from God, and you are not your own? For you were bought at a price; therefore, glorify God in your body and in your Spirit, which is God's" (1 Corinthians 6:19-20).

It's in the imagination of men and in their thought life where Satan challenges God. We have heard it all before in Genesis and the Wilderness. "Hath God said? Does God know? Is there knowledge in the highest? Does God see?" And quite often, Satan deceives us into thinking God doesn't see. Thus, the importance of the 'Helmet of Salvation.'

If we have the mind of the flesh, then we're going to reap corruption. But if we have the intention of the Spirit, then we're going to obtain life, joy, and peace in the Holy Spirit. These Strongholds are wrong thoughts and beliefs, arguments, contradicting God. They hold on to every high thing that exalts itself against the knowledge of God.

At some point, even God will have had enough of all these foolish and prideful people. "And even as they did not like to retain God in their knowledge, God gave them over to a reprobate mind, to do those things which are not convenient" (Romans 1:28). We know the end of the story because we have read the book and personally know the author. God will return with all the Saints to redeem the Title Deed of the Earth from Satan.

DO ALL ROADS LEAD TO GOD?

Satan's greatest weapon is man's ignorance of God's Word! Additionally, half of the truth is the worst part of the lie. With every temptation, there is a lie involved. (1) The Prove It Lie, (2) The "For It Is Written" Lie, and (3) The Short Cut Lie. The devil deceived Eve in the garden with these lies while Jesus was victorious in the wilderness. We must learn how to use the Word of God to overcome Satan.

The problem with half-truths is that when we believe them, we receive the consequences of that decision. Half-truths are enticing, pleasant, and a more natural path to take. Satan told Eve half of God's truth, deceiving her into partaking of the fruit of the tree. That decision resulted in the fall of man and the curses pronounced upon Satan, Adam, and Eve. Everyone today is experiencing the ramifications of their decision each day we live on earth.

Satan later tried this deception on Jesus in the wilderness, but Jesus wisely used the WORD to overcome the temptations. Jesus replies to every lie by speaking the Word of Truth; "For it is written . . . Worship the Lord thy God" (Matthew 4:10).

There are so many perplexing questions facing us in life. Such as, "Which came first the chicken or the egg?" GOD came first, creating the chicken with the ability to lay eggs. Here is an insightful question asked of me, "If God is so great, can He make a rock too heavy for Him to pick up? WELL YES! Because He is GOD. But then He could reduce the weight and toss the stone across the universe. Silly little "Got You" Questions that only comfort those who would debate and deny God anyway. God doesn't play that game!

The greatest and most deceptive half-truth conceived by man is that "ALL ROADS LEAD TO GOD." This eternally destructive lie states that since God is love, and you're a good person, God will never send you to hell. The whole and complete truth are that all roads do lead to God but for distinct reasons and different ends: believers for their rewards and non-believers for judgment.

Furthermore, God doesn't send anyone to hell. We alone choose between heaven or hell according to our belief in or rejection of Jesus Christ. Those who accepted Jesus as their Lord and Savior will receive eternal life. Those who deny Christ will be judged, and by that decision alone, be separated from God for all eternity. Free choice can either be a gift or a curse. Recall the Fall and stay obedient to God's Truth.

I think Alice-in-Wonderland said, "If you don't know where you are going, any road will get you there." I am sure she was referring to the rabbit hole roads in her fairy tale. Maybe this is what people are miss quoting when they say, "All roads lead to Heaven." Be aware of this kind of Half-Truth-Thinking.

If you fall for a half-truth, you have taken on the complete lie. Remember, sin has ramifications on the individual, their circle of family, and friends. Sin has consequences that affect us momentarily, seasonally, generationally, and in some cases, eternally. Justly, we do reap what we sow.

THE SHORT CUT LIE IS QUID PRO QUO

Matthew gives an account of the Temptation of Jesus in the wilderness. In using the Short cut lie, Satan's offer was that he would give Jesus all the kingdoms of the world if He would bow down to him. Then Jesus said to him, "Away with you, Satan! For it is written, 'You shall worship the LORD your God, and Him only you shall serve'" (Matthew 4:10).

Jesus had come to save the world and to repurchase it from the grip and control of Satan. But it would take a horrible death on the Cross to accomplish that. Satan was essentially offering Jesus (QUID PRO QUO) a shortcut. "You don't have to suffer and go to the cross just compromise, and I'll give you everything right now," Jesus responded in each case by quoting scripture and by resisting the temptation. We cast the final vote to sin or not to sin. No one can make that decision for us-regardless of the pressures we may be facing.

God does promise to deliver us when tempted. However, He does not guarantee that trials will no longer be part of our life. Satan knows our areas of weakness. If we have fallen in one area before, rest assured that he will come at us again from the same angle. Jesus encourages us: "Be thou faithful unto death, and I will give thee a crown of life" (Revelation 2:10).

God always limits the power of every temptation so that we can overcome it. He supplies a way to escape through it. The Holy Spirit guides us through the trials, not around or over them. He is on our team throughout every test. The Lord doesn't lead us into temptations but will see us through them as we trust Him to do so.

Temptation itself is not a sin. Keep in mind that we are not responsible for what flashes through our minds.

Our responsibility is to control the things that dominate our thoughts. Jesus dealt with temptations in all areas of life, but without sin.

Just like feeling angry is not sin, but, if not dealt with, can be a temptation that needs immediate attention. It is what you do with that anger that counts. James reminds us: "But every man is tempted, when he is drawn away of his lust, and enticed. Then when lust hath conceived, it bringeth forth sin: and sin, when it is finished, bringeth forth death" (James 1:14-15). What you do with the temptation is what counts!

Surely, God was not disappointed during the temptations of Christ in the wilderness. Point being the attraction is not a sin unless we embrace it. We confuse how we feel with how God thinks about us. The Bible assures us that God rewards those who are tempted-if they persevere: James 1:12 "Blessed [is] the man that endureth temptation: for when he is tried, he shall receive the crown of life, which the Lord hath promised to them that love him."

Therefore, you must deny yourself and take up your Cross. Someone said the Cross in your life, is often where your will, crosses God's will. You must follow Jesus, and you must not let anything stand in the way of following Him. Anything that would stand in the way, you must deny yourself in that area of life. The Lord will always put His finger on what it is in our life -that specific thing that is keeping us from following Him. He will use the trials and temptations of life to allow us to be complete in Him, wanting nothing.

THE THREE LIES THAT DID NOT STUMBLE JESUS

Our best example of how to resist temptation is how Jesus endured the enemy. After fasting forty days and forty nights, Jesus was led up by the Spirit into the wilderness to be tempted by the devil, and He answered every temptation of Satan with the Word. David wrote, "Your word I have hidden in my heart that I might not sin against You" (Psalm 119:11).

Strength in overcoming the wicked one comes through the Word of God. And then, our victory is through prayer. Paul says, "praying with all prayer and the Word along with supplication in the Spirit…" (Ephesians 6:13-18). Again, the real power against the enemy and the world is prayer and supplication (petition) in the Spirit. As you stand in the name of Jesus, you will come to know, through God's Word and in prayer, the power and the victory over the temptation that is trying to pull you down into a pit. James exhorts us, "Therefore, submit to God. Resist the devil, and he will flee from you" (James 4:7).

When tempted in the wilderness, Jesus used the Word to overcome the enemy. With every temptation, He proclaimed, "For it is written," and He was victorious in rebuking Satan and obeying the will of His Father.

THE PROVE IT LIE: Here in Matthew 4:1-11, we see the account of Jesus' temptation by Satan. The first temptation from Satan suggested that "If you are the Son of God, command that these stones become bread" (verse 3). This lie was the temptation to allow the flesh to rule over the Spirit.

But He answered and said, "It is written, "Man shall not live by bread alone, but by every word that proceeds from the mouth of God" (verse 4).

THE "FOR IT IS WRITTEN" LIE: The second temptation was when Satan took Him up to the pinnacle of the temple and was told to throw Himself down and let the angels save Him. Here Satan took a verse out of context and tried to get Jesus to test God inappropriately.

Jesus said to him, "It is written again, 'You shall not tempt the LORD your God" (verse 7).

THE SHORT CUT LIE: The third temptation Satan offered was that he would give Jesus all the kingdoms of the world if He would bow down to him.

Then Jesus said to him, "Away with you, Satan! For it is written, 'You shall worship the LORD your God, and Him only you shall serve'" (verse 10).

Jesus refused the devil's temptations because God sent Him to fulfill His purpose. But it would take a horrible death on the Cross to accomplish that. Satan was essentially offering Jesus a shortcut to fulfilling His mission. "You don't have to suffer and go to the Cross, just compromise, and I'll give you everything right now," Jesus responded in each case resisting the temptation using the Word of God.

Jesus was to be obedient to God's will and buying into Satan's short cut lie would defeat His plan of salvation. Nothing but the Cross could save humanity. Short cut lies present themselves to Believers in this world; however, ask: "What would Jesus do?"

BE DOERS OF THE WORD

We can incorporate the "For it is Written" spiritual weapon as Jesus did in the wilderness. However, putting this into our war chest comes at a cost. The cost is the time spent reading, studying, meditating, praying, confessing, declaring, and applying GOD'S WORD in our spiritual lives. How can we quote that which is not available? Timothy urges us to "Study to shew thyself approved unto God, a workman that needeth not to be ashamed, rightly dividing the word of truth" (2 Timothy 2:15).

The Word is a powerful piece of armor, "and the sword of the Spirit, which is the word of God" (Ephesians 6:17b). This sword is our offensive weapon, and it protects us from lies when we trust in the truth of God's Word. We use the sword to attack our enemies with the Word.

Also, it's the only weapon we used OFFENSIVELY AND DEFENSIVELY. Find a passage of scripture that pertains to your need, apply its principles to the promise, and stand firm in the faith. In using this spiritual tool, we will become more like Jesus as we put on the mind of Christ and reflect His Image from glory to glory, AMEN.

Since we are to be doers of the Word and not hearers only, now's a proper time to put into practice the teaching of Christ. Let's not make the mistakes Adam and Eve did in the Garden. Best to respond to our temptations as Jesus did. Remember, we have put on the mind of Christ, so we should think, act, and answer the same way Jesus did.

The following are a few lies that we meet during our lifetime. I will start us off, but I encourage you to continue with your list. Only you and God knows what temptations you face.

> NOTE: These Scriptures are promises for your application. Praying and speaking scripture are two of your most potent weapons.

THE LIE: The devil tricked me, and so I did it.

IT IS WRITTEN: "Therefore submit to God. Resist the devil, and he will flee from you. Draw near to God, and He will draw near to you. Cleanse your hands, you sinners; and purify your hearts, you double-minded" (James 4:7-8).

IT IS WRITTEN: "You are of God, little children, and have overcome them because He who is in you is greater than he who is in the world" (1 John 4:4).

IT IS WRITTEN: "We know that whoever is born of God does not sin, but he who has been born of God keeps himself, and the wicked one does not touch him" (1 John 5:18).

IT IS WRITTEN: "Put on the whole armor of God, that you may be able to stand against the wiles of the devil" (Ephesians 6:11).

THE LIE: I will never change.

IT IS WRITTEN: "Then said Jesus to those Jews which believed on him, If ye continue in my word, then are ye my disciples indeed; And ye shall know the truth, and the truth shall make you free" (John 8:31-32).

THE LIE: This trial will never end.

IT IS WRITTEN: "There has no temptation taken you, but such as is common to man: but God is faithful, who will not suffer you to be tempted above that ye are able; but will with the temptation also make a way to escape, that ye may be able to bear it" (1 Corinthians 10:13).

IT IS WRITTEN: "In this, you greatly rejoice, though now for a little while, if need be, you have been grieved by various trials, that the genuineness of your faith, being much more precious than gold that perishes, though it is tested by fire, may be found to praise, honor, and glory at the revelation of Jesus Christ" (1 Peter 1:6-7).

THE LIE: My friends are not going to influence me because I'm strong enough to handle it.

IT IS WRITTEN: "He who walks with wise men will be wise, but the companion of fools will be destroyed" (Proverbs 13:20).

IT IS WRITTEN: "For a righteous man may fall seven times and rise again, but the wicked shall fall by calamity" (Proverbs 24:16).

THE LIE: I don't have enough faith.

IT IS WRITTEN: "So then faith cometh by hearing, and hearing by the word of God" (Romans 10:17).

IT IS WRITTEN: "Therefore we also, since we are surrounded by so great a cloud of witnesses, let us lay aside every weight and the sin which so easily ensnares us, and let us run with endurance the race that is set before us, looking unto Jesus, the author, and finisher of our faith, who for the joy that was set before Him endured the cross, despising the shame, and has sat down at the right hand of the throne of God" (Hebrews 12:1-2).

IT IS WRITTEN: "Reaching Forth Unto Those Things Which Are Before, I Press Toward The Mark For The Prize Of The High Calling Of God In Christ Jesus…," (Philippians 3:7-14).

THE LIE: I can't control what I think about my thought life seems to influence every aspect of my being.

IT IS WRITTEN: "I can do all things through Christ which strengtheneth me" (Philippians 4:13).

IT IS WRITTEN: "Casting down imaginations, and every high thing that exalteth itself against the knowledge of God and bringing into captivity every thought to the obedience of Christ" (2 Corinthians 10:5).

IT IS WRITTEN: "And be not conformed to this world: but transformed by the renewing of your mind, that you may prove what is that good, and acceptable, and perfect will of God" (Romans 12:2).

IT IS WRITTEN: "That ye put off concerning the former conversation the old man, which is corrupt according to the deceitful lusts; And be renewed in the spirit of your mind; And that ye put on the new man, which after God is created in righteousness and true holiness" (Ephesians 4:22-24).

IT IS WRITTEN: "Finally, brethren, whatever things are true, whatever things are noble, whatever things are just, whatever things are pure, whatever things are lovely, whatever things are of good report if there is any virtue and if there is anything praiseworthy—meditate on these things" (Philippians 4:8).

A PROMISE

"No weapon that is formed against thee shall prosper, and every tongue that shall rise against thee in judgment thou shalt condemn. This is the heritage of the servants of the LORD, and their righteousness is of me, saith the LORD" (Isaiah 54:17).

A PRAYER

Dear Father, Your Word says that no weapon formed against me shall prosper. Therefore, I declare that no weapon formed against me prospers this day or any day to come in Jesus' name. Your Word says that trouble will not arise a second time (Nahum 1:9). Therefore, I declare that Satan cannot make trouble for me again, in this manner, as he did in the past in Jesus' name. I say all these prayers carried out and brought to pass by trusting you through faith and expectation in the name of Jesus, AMEN.

7

THE EMPTY NETS OF SUCCESS

Jesus said to Peter, "Let me get into your boat." Jesus begins to speak to the multitudes that had gathered on the shoreline. Peter is thinking, "Here is Jesus in my boat, and I've failed Him; I've let Him down. I started to become His disciple; I even saw miracles.

This story of Peter is about a man who learned from his failure. And how success happened because of a simple thing. It happened when Jesus came aboard his little boat and gave directions that he followed. And that is where we will find success in our lives when we let Jesus be in control. We will all have failures, but we will learn more from our failures than our successes. When we have partial success, it's because we only partially obeyed.

Consequently, the reason Peter was pulling up empty nets was that he was outside God's will. If you know God has called you to do a sure thing, yet you refuse to do it, you are miserable and frustrated, and you're pulling up empty net after empty net. It is time to return to your first love and do what God has told you to do, and you will be where you ought to be.

Jesus had said to Peter on another occasion, when he was out fishing, "Follow me, and I will make you fishers of men." We read that they ditched their nets, left their boats and businesses to follow Jesus. But somewhere along the way something happened, and they stopped following him after they had started. So, here in Luke 5 is the second time Jesus had asked them to become fishers of men.

Jesus could have used Peter as a sermon illustration. "Look at this man, he began to follow me and turned back, and he is pulling up empty nets. Might I say, let this man be an example to you." However, He turned to Peter and said, "Let's go fishing, but this time let's do it my way."

Jesus had said to launch out into the deep, but every fisher knew that the time to fish was at night and in the shallow waters, not in the deep waters in the daytime. Peter might have been thinking that we are fishermen, professionals, and we know these matters. You might be high on spiritual issues, but we are the experts when it comes to fishing. However, Peter says, "At your word, we will let down the nets." If Peter had not obeyed the first seemingly insignificant command, he would never have taken part in a miracle.

So, he went ahead and did it, to humor Jesus. Of course, he and those with him caught so many fish that their boats began to sink. As the boats were sinking, it began to sink into Peter who Jesus was. He knew Jesus wasn't just a man, but that He was the Messiah. But as he recognized Jesus for who He is, Peter also saw himself for who he was. He said, "Depart from me, for I am a sinful man, O Lord!"

Whenever we get a vision of who Jesus is, it will always give us a realistic perspective of who we are, as well. We do not see the truth about ourselves until we see ourselves in His light. Seeing ourselves in His light always brings conviction.

It is the little things God would have us be faithful in because if we aren't, we will never go out into the deep. So, we must first start with what we know is the will of God for us at this very moment in time and do it! Partial obedience will never fulfill God's purpose.

Patience and timing are critical when waiting on God to use us. Sometimes God has the right person at the right place but at the wrong time. Too early, sometimes too late. Moses is an excellent example of the importance of timing. He wanted to do something for his people, but he was impatient, 40 years too early. If we do it God's way, in God's timing, our nets will be breaking as well, because He has directed our path.

Looking over Moses' life, we find that he spent 40 years in Pharaoh's court finding out that he was a somebody,

40 years in the backside of the desert finding out that he was a nobody. Then he spent 40 years in the wilderness finding out what God can do with a somebody that see's he's a nobody.

Now, after the net was full, what was Peter's reaction? He said, "Depart from me for I am a sinful man." What a way to say thanks. He was humbled; God had revealed himself to Peter in a realm he could understand. Peter had seen other miracles; he had seen his mother in law healed. But Peter knew of the impossibility of this happening by chance or circumstance, and he knew that it was God working. And it was God working for him personally, and it humbled him out.

God has made allowances for our failures; that is why he died on the cross for us. We all have fallen short of the glory of God. When we fail, not if, but when we fail, if we learn from that experience, it will help us out the next time we face it or something like it.

But He is still saying, "Follow me and I'll make you fishers of men. Let me on board, let me give you direction, let me take control, and everything will change." As we go out to serve him, as we go out in life, it's essential that we let him on board and let him be in control and let him be captain of our ship.

Make Him Lordship in every area of life. He has set before us opportunities to serve him, to make a difference, opportunities to catch men alive. In closing, Jesus said to Peter, "From this day on, you will catch men alive."

GOD REWARDS OUR OBEDIENCE

Let's look at what happened when the disciples obeyed Jesus' instructions. "Put out into the deep water and let down your nets for a catch" (Luke 5:4).

Life is a composite of decisions. Where we are today is the result of choices we made in the past and today's decisions determine where we will be tomorrow.

THE RESULTS OF THE DISCIPLES' OBEDIENCE TO JESUS' Instruction:

- Two boats full of fish, nets were breaking
- Peter was a part of and took part in a miracle of God
- Peter saw himself as he had never seen himself before
- Others received the benefits of the miracle
- Peter's concept of God changed
- God changed the disciple's vocation
- God broke their hearts and instilled the correct idea of Jesus
- Jesus became a living reality for them.

You need to know what you want in life before you can make well-informed decisions. Also, you must factor in God's will, promises and purpose. Will this decision glorify God and help prove my life's purpose? Having a good sense of yourself and your relationship with God makes the whole decision process more manageable.

PROMISES

"Blessed [is] the man that endureth temptation: for when he is tried, he shall receive the crown of life, which the Lord hath promised to them that love him" (James 1:12).

Jesus says, "Behold! I am coming quickly, and My Reward is with Me, to Render (Reward) to every man according to what he has DONE"(Revelation 22:12).

A PRAYER

Dear God, help me to put off pride—and put on humility. Help me to put off my critical nature—and put on the acceptance of others. Help me to put off worrying—and put on the peace that comes through trusting You. Help me bring my thoughts under control by putting on the mind of Christ. In Jesus's name-AMEN

"Search me, O God, and know my heart: try me, and know my thoughts: And see if there be any wicked way in me and lead me in the way everlasting" (Psalm 139:23-24).

"Dear God, thank you for loving me, saving me, and protecting me. Give me the strength to press on toward the high calling for which you have apprehended me. May my light shine bright as you receive the glory as you transform me into the image of Christ. Might I do your will as you guide me and instruct me daily? Give me faith to believe and wisdom to obey Your Word throughout my journey. In Jesus' name-AMEN!"

8

PRAYING SCRIPTURE EMPOWERS OUR PRAYER LIFE

"Now this is the confidence that we have in Him, that if we ask anything according to His will, He hears us. And if we know that He hears us, whatever we ask, we know that we have the petitions that we have asked of Him" (1 John 5:14-15).

Praying and seeking God should be a top priority in the believer's life. Prayer is mentioned over 500 times in the Scriptures. Everyone can exercise this fantastic resource. It's a ministry for many, and the most crucial activity afforded a believer.

Incredibly, we each have a high priority connection directly into the Throne Room of the Universe! It is bizarre to realize that this astonishing resource is so available and so rarely used. It is unquestionably the most potent weapon we could have.

What a powerful spiritual weapon prayer is. In this spiritual warfare, prayer is often the deciding factor in the spiritual battle. "Praying with all prayer and supplication in the Spirit, watching with all perseverance and supplication for all the saints; and for pray for me, [Paul says,] that utterance may be given unto me, that I may open my mouth boldly, to make known the mystery of the gospel" (Ephesians 6:18-19).

As we mature in our faith and knowledge of God's Word, we often find ourselves praying familiar verses and promises of Scripture in our prayers. This form helps us pray God's will, reminding (although He is all-knowing) Him of the promises He has made to us, which strengthens our prayers.

Praying the promises is a practice to help center our attention on His Word. We turn these promises into prayers, asking God to provide for what He has promised, through Jesus, so that we can abide with God.

- When we pray God's Word—our prayers become Swords in our hands that defeat the powers of darkness.
- So powerful and sharper than any double-edged sword that will reveal the thoughts and attitudes of the heart.
- His words do not return empty but carry out God's desired purpose.

- The presence and power of the Holy Spirit aid us in the situations we cover with Prayer.

So vital is praying God's will in fulfilling our purpose and ministry. When we add Scriptures, we can be sure that God will hear our spiritual concerns. Including Scripture in our prayer life will help confirm we're praying God's will because His Word is His will. When we pray it, He hears and addresses our prayers.

"This is the confidence we have in approaching God: that if we ask anything according to his will, he hears us. And if we know that he hears us—whatever we ask— we know that we have what we asked of him" (1 John 5:14).

PRAYER IS THE GREATEST PRIVILEGE OF ALL

The main essence of prayer is talking to God and listening to Him, though there are many other sides a person can incorporate into their prayer life. Maintaining an active prayer life will help you achieve victory when going through trials and tribulations in life. Talking to God will help you overcome temptations that come your way.

God's Word supplies many prayers throughout the Bible to prove His love and mercy toward believers. These prayers intercede for us and are examples for us to consider in our prayer life. God's prayer for us expands the volume of Scripture. Read the Book of Psalms and pray them to God for yourself.

Jesus gives us guidance on how to pray in The Lord's Prayer (Some refer to it as The Model Prayer) in Matthew 6:8-13. However, in John Chapter 17, we find the Prayer of Jesus, where He prays for Himself, His disciples, and all believers.

The most important prayer you can ever pray is (The Sinner's Prayer), the one that invites Jesus into your heart to forgive your sins. God's summation of our Prayer Life in 1 Thessalonians 5:16-18 is a remarkable exhortation! "Rejoice always, pray without ceasing, in everything give thanks; for this is the will of God in Christ Jesus for you."

THE BENEFITS OF MAINTAINING A CONSISTENT PRAYER LIFE

To whom should we pray?

The typical pattern of prayer and worship involves the unique roles of each member of the Trinity:
- We address our prayers to the Father (the Source)
- We pray in the name of Jesus Christ (the Mediator)
- We pray with the power of the Holy Spirit (the Enabler).

How do we make prayer a part of our everyday life? We can learn from three things that Jesus did:

A CERTAIN TIME: Jesus got up early in the morning to spend time with His Heavenly Father. For prayer to work, we should do the same. Make a daily appointment with God and keep it. "Very early in the morning, while it was still dark, Jesus got up, left the house and went off to a solitary place, where he prayed" (Mark 1:35).

A CERTAIN PLACE: Jesus had a prayer place. Your prayer place needs to be an undistracted environment where you can pray out loud and perhaps have some worship music playing in the background.

A CERTAIN PLAN: Go into your prayer time with a plan. If it changes, that's fine. When Jesus taught His disciples how to pray, He gave His disciples a prayer outline. We call it the Lord's Prayer.

Jesus suggests to His prayer warriors, "But thou, when thou prays, enter into thy closet, and when thou hast shut thy door, pray to thy Father which is in secret; and thy Father who sees in secret shall reward thee openly" (Matthew 6:6).

- Our intimate relationship strengthens with Jesus Christ when we spend time with Him in Prayer.
- Our Perspective (point of view) and Perception (awareness) of who God is grows as we discover what He is like; we realize His vastness and greatness, strengthening our maturity in our walk with Him.
- We are going to have a Positive faith attitude, not a positive mind. You will positively know that your faith is active. We are going to see things God's way, and we are going to begin to trust Him in ways we never trusted Him before.
- There is going to be a Purifying Process in our heart as we begin to make prayer a priority. Purity in our life will bring power to persevere and proclaim as Paul does here: "I press toward the mark for the prize of the high calling of God in Christ Jesus" (Philippians 3:14).
- We are going to develop a Passion for obedience. When you begin to pray, God does

something in your heart, creating a passion for compliance leading to maturity.

- The Pressures of our life are going to dissipate, and we are going to begin experiencing a sense of peace with God, leading to peace in God, which we hadn't been able to experience before.
- The Provision for our needs. We are going to see God as the Provider for our needs, and we will begin to rely upon Him.
- Prayer is the Pathway to our spiritual growth. Something is going to happen in us and through us as God develops His purpose in our lives. From glory to glory conformed into His image. "Now the Lord is that Spirit: and where the Spirit of the Lord is, there is liberty. But we all, with open face beholding as in a glass the glory of the Lord, are changed into the same image from glory to glory, even as by the Spirit of the Lord" (2 Corinthians 3:17-18).
- We will experience higher Power in our spiritual life, in our devotional life, in our witness to others than ever before. We find such strength in the Holy Spirit and by "putting on the whole armor of God…," Ephesians 6:10-18) because, "Though we walk in the flesh, we do not war after the flesh: (For the weapons of our warfare are not carnal, but

mighty through God to the pulling down of strongholds") (2 Corinthians 10:3-4).

The Apostle Luke tells us of this spiritual power provided by God, "But ye shall receive power, after that the Holy Ghost has come upon you: and ye shall be witnesses unto me both in Jerusalem, and in all Judaea, and Samaria, and unto the uttermost part of the earth" (Acts 1:8).

- Something is going to happen to your entire life. You are going to experience productivity, enabling you to produce the life God has called you to live. Such a life is fruitful in your spiritual life and your ministry for God.

Incorporating and relying on Scripture to bring about productivity according to God's will, dramatically increases our success. Finally, after Paul tells us to put on the whole armor of God, he closes this section of Scripture by urging us to pray always. "Praying always with all prayer and supplication in the Spirit and watching thereunto with all perseverance and supplication for all saints" Ephesians 6: 18).

A PROMISE

"Now this is the confidence that we have in Him, that if we ask anything according to His will, He hears us. And if we know that He hears us, whatever we ask, we know that we have the petitions that we have asked of Him." (John 5:14-15)

A PRAYER

Father, I confess that so often I have failed the test: that I've allowed the flesh to rule over the spirit. Forgive me, Lord, and cleanse me. Let me be governed by Your Holy Spirit and by Your eternal Word of truth. IN JESUS; NAME, AMEN

9

MORE PRECIOUS THAN GOLD

"It is good for me that I was afflicted,
that I may learn Your statutes."
(Psalm 119:71)

God is setting up His eternal kingdom, and He uses the fiery trials of life to build our faith, mature us, lead us, deliver us, and develop character within us. Foremost, tests are one-way God's plan can merge with His purpose for our lives.

So, it's critical to understand the purpose of trials so to know what to do, how to do it, when to do it, why we are doing it, what happens if we don't do it and what are our rewards for doing it right? A great insight is we embrace trials while resisting temptations. We must get it right here on earth, so to be right when we arrive in heaven. Remember, there are no do-overs once we leave this life behind.

God desires us to embrace trials while resisting temptations.

Discerning the origin of trials helps formulate the proper response to them and uncovers God's purposes behind them. Are they from the devil, our carnal mind, imposed by a fallen world and the people around us, or something God would have us embrace? Discovering the purpose of trials, how to overcome them, how to be obedient during them, how to grow because of them, and which promises can I apply to them, will lay the foundation to "... Count it all joy" when these fiery trials appear.

One purpose of a trial is to know what is in your heart. Not that God doesn't already know. The prophet Jeremiah reaffirms, "The heart is deceitful above all things, and desperately wicked; Who can know it? I, the LORD, search the heart, I test the mind" (Jeremiah 17:9-10). God's testing helps us to understand ourselves and to know our limitations and our weaknesses, so we will learn to trust in God and not in ourselves.

During trials, it is challenging to realize that God will lead us step by step through them. There are so many things in our lives that God needs to deal with, but He cannot deal with them until they surface, and testing will do that to allow us to see the truth. We need to be humble. We cannot allow pride to rule in our hearts. Pride will always keep us from seeing the truth about ourselves. Always remember that God hates the proud. Pride is a great enemy to you. It will lie to you, and it can destroy you. But "humble yourself in the sight of the Lord, and He will lift you up" (James 4:10).

Trials bring us closer to God, where we learn to grow and where we see the power and the love of God manifested. It's there where you come into a deeper relationship with God. James tells us to, "But let patience have its perfect work, that you may be perfect and complete, lacking nothing" (James 1:4).

Furthermore, an incredible purpose for trials is to mold us into the image of Jesus Christ. They also bring you into maturity as you learn lessons from trials. God would have us to grow up and become mature. Patience is one of the main ways that produces wisdom and maturity.

This word patience does not describe a passive waiting but an active endurance. Perseverance is "the frame of mind which endures." You don't become patient by trying to be patient. It isn't something that we receive as a gift of the Holy Spirit. It is something that God has chosen to develop in us through trials. We don't like to hear that; we would rather have instant patience. "Lord, please give me patience, and I want it right now."

Believers do everything possible to avoid trials. We try to avoid them like the plague. Interestingly, they are referred to by Peter as being more precious than gold. There often comes a time when we look back upon a trial and bless God for it, rather than murmur to Him about it as we did before.

God's Word is full of instructions for us to follow. I AM THAT I AM. He has declared! Thus, whatever we need in life, He has a promise with the way to apply it and prosper. Believers can count on God's grace and mercy in everything that comes their way.

The Apostle Paul exhorts us in Romans, "I beseech you therefore, brethren, by the mercies of God, that you present your bodies a living sacrifice, holy, acceptable to God, which is your reasonable service. And do not be conformed to this world, but be transformed by the renewing of your mind, that you may prove what that good and acceptable and perfect will of God" (Romans 12:1-2).

"That you may prove what that good and acceptable and perfect will of God…" What a glorious promise! We often don't know what to do in a situation. There are so many things in life that we don't know what the correct path is to take. We lack wisdom. It's beautiful to be able to come to God and ask for wisdom and realize that He will give to all believers freely. The wisest thing that you can ever do is to seek the knowledge of God.

James tells us, "If any of you lacks wisdom, let him ask of God, who gives to all liberally and without reproach, and it will be given to him" (James 1:5).

Trials bring a necessary season to seek wisdom from God. We often don't know how much we need understanding until our time of difficulty. During a test, we need to see if it is something God wants us to eliminate from our lives, is it a lesson we need to learn, or is the devil attacking our faith in God? Wisdom must discern between the three, perseverance to get through it, and trust in God is knowing He is with us.

Wisdom is much more than knowledge, and believers need to seek it with their whole heart. Knowledge is raw information, but wisdom knows how to use it. Someone once said that "knowledge is the ability to take things apart, but wisdom is the ability to put things together."

"But let him ask in faith, with no doubting, for he who doubts is like a wave of the sea driven and tossed by the wind" (James 1:6).

Sometimes we lack unwavering faith. We doubt that God will work in us and help us through this trial. James tells us that we should ask in faith, nothing wavering. He tells us that wavering hope is a weak faith. Unwavering faith is sure and founded on the promises of God.

Believers waver on many issues because they do not know the will of the Lord on a specific matter. But we must remember that our request for wisdom must be made like any other request – in faith, without doubting God's ability or desire to give us His knowledge.

We must come in faith and must ask in faith. We must pray for God's guidance with no doubting. Scripture tells us the one who doubts and lacks confidence should not expect to receive anything from the Lord. This lack of faith and trust in God also shows that we don't have a strong enough foundation and will cause us to be unstable in all our ways.

"For I know the thoughts that I think toward you, says the LORD, thoughts of peace and not of evil, to give you a future and a hope."

(Jeremiah 29:11 NKJV).

PROMISES

"There hath no temptation taken you, but such as is common to man: but God is faithful, who will not suffer you to be tempted above that ye are able; but will with the temptation also make a way to escape, that ye may be able to bear it" (1 Corinthians 10:13).

"I can do all things through Christ which strengtheneth me" (Philippians 4:13).

"Submit yourselves therefore to God. Resist the devil, and he will flee from you" (James 4:7).

"Ye are of God, little children, and have overcome them: because greater is he that is in you, than he that is in the world" (1 John 4:4).

A PRAYER

When Making a Difficult Decision

Dear Lord, the decision I must make will affect my life profoundly, and that makes me tense. Calm my mind. Show me what to do and how to do it. Help me listen to your answer and know the answer when it comes. Above all, help me see that it will happen. In Jesus' name. Amen.

God is our refuge and strength, a very present help in trouble. (Psalm 46:1)

10

GOD'S STILL SMALL VOICE

Have you ever argued with God knowing you will never win? Or making promises in the Spirit that your flesh refuses to fulfill? Well, a crazy thing happened on the way to eternity. I lost an argument with God. Can you believe that? There I was in the back of my semitrailer, making a delivery, and arguing with God. Attempting to negotiate terms with Him knowing quite well, He doesn't play that game.

I was trying to negotiate the terms of dating my checkout girl at the grocery store. I had been going there buying one item at a time to talk to her. Never having the nerve to ask her out, I just kept going in, hoping God would open the door. Maybe He might give me the backbone to pursue this desire. I tried bargaining with Him explaining how great of an addition she would be to His kingdom, and I would help bring this about for Him.

The argument with God in my semitrailer had us both standing our ground. Telling Him, I was going to ask her out the next time I went shopping, and God was saying absolutely, NOT! As we went around and around, I stepped off the back of my trailer, landing on my back. Looking up to heaven, I heard His still small voice saying, "Do I have your attention now?" He did; however, there are differences between hearing, listening, and doing.

Many times, my flesh pondered, "how can I live for the Lord and still get my way?" Short answer, I can't! Nevertheless, I still disobeyed Him by going to see her, and this time, I would ask her out.

Upon my next visit, she was so excited to see me, which encouraged me to ask the question. Though her delight was not because of me, it was her last day at work. She was moving back east and just wanted to say goodbye. So much for our future together. God decided that if I would not listen and obey Him concerning this temptation, He'd remove it from my life. His ways are not our ways, and the sooner we surrender to God's will, the easier and quicker it is to receive the right promise.

A LESSON FROM THE WOODSHED

Throughout my walk with my Lord, I have been a hypocrite and a big offender of the Short Cut Lie. Always finding myself halfway between here and there with God. I had often pondered this question, "How could I obey God in my backslidden state but disobey when I was seeking Him with my whole heart?"

I'm sure it has much to do about listening. God chastens us because He loves us and wants us to return to our first love. God will work through us for His glory, no matter the condition of our hearts. The scriptures are full of examples of how He used evil and sinful men for His Purpose.

Often God has tried to speak to me through a still small voice, and I didn't listen. Such the case with my argument with Him in the back of my trailer. Subsequently, He brought the hammer down on me to get my attention. All because His whispering didn't penetrate my heart.

Sometimes God speaks through earthquakes, wind, and fire. We remember those times and expect Him to always talk in those ways. But most generally, when God speaks to us, He speaks in a still small voice. If we are spiritually sensitive, our hearts will hear the voice of God.

By not being silent, we often miss the voice of God because we are expecting Him to speak in some great thunderous tone. We need to get our hearts quiet before God. We must believe the still small voice of God within guides us assures us of His love and assures us of His Purpose. It's that even faint voice within needing our attention and obedience. Then we will receive the strength and help from God when He speaks to us.

AFTERTHOUGHTS

I AM all you will ever need. I AM to you whatever your need may be. And it is interesting, as God declared, "I AM," He was speaking of that eternal aspect of His character. He is the Eternal One.

The name of God is a verb "to be." "The Becoming One" is named Yahweh, as God becomes to you whatever your need might be. "I am your peace, your strength, your help. I am your guide. I am your righteousness. I am your salvation. I am your hope." How beautiful that is. "The Becoming One is named Yahweh, The Becoming One," as God becomes to you whatever your need might be.

"For all the promises of God in Him are Yes, and in Him Amen, to the glory of God through us."

(2 Corinthians 1:20)

EACH DAY IS A DAY CLOSER TO ETERNITY.

TIME IS RUNNING OUT.

"God's promises will expire (in the twinkling of an eye) between our last breath and our entrance into eternity."

A PROMISE

"Blessed [is] the man that endureth temptation: for when he is tried, he shall receive the crown of life, which the Lord hath promised to them that love him." (James 1:12)

A PRAYER

"May the LORD bless you and keep you; The LORD to make His face shine upon you and be gracious to you; The LORD lift His countenance upon you, And give you peace."

AMEN

ABOUT THE AUTHOR

SELECTIVE BIOGRAPHY ON AUTHOR BRAD WYRICK

Brad's Purpose as an author is to help people connect with God through the Truth of God's Word. He has a passion for New Believers in Christ and has written and taught Bible Studies for over thirty years. Hearing God's voice, pursuing God's purpose, applying God's truth, and conforming into the image of Christ is what each of his books will always aim to communicate.

Wyrick grew up in California during the 1960s and 1970s and took part in both the Hippie and Jesus movements. One of the reasons Brad is especially grateful for God's forgiveness is because of the former life God reconciled. Even though Brad accepted Christ in a church tent in California (Calvary Chapel) in 1969, Brad himself will admit he was far from being a saint during many seasons of his life.

Since rededicating his life to the Lord in 1978, Brad has had a love for and voracious appetite for the Word of God. He moved into a discipleship home run by Christians (The Lord's House) and spent a year there studying the Bible and building a foundation in Christ.

Continuing to pursue his Purpose in Life, he then attended Calvary Chapel Bible College in the mountains of Arrowhead in California. Brad taught New Believer Classes at Calvary Chapel Costa Mesa and the Vineyard Church in Newport Beach. Also, leading Kinship groups and Small groups over the years.

BOOKS PUBLISHED BY BRAD WYRICK

- *In and Out of the World, 1977*
- *Son Runners, 2017*
- *God's Promises, Principles, and Provisions, 2017*
- *God's Past Promises Meet our Present Response, 2018*
- *How to Discover, Design & Apply Your God-Given Life*
- *Mission, 2018*
- *# "No Room in The Inn?", 2019*
- *I AM The Promise Keeper, 2020*

Author Page: *www.amazon.com/Brad-Wyrick/*
Follow Me Group: *https://www.facebook.com/wyrick.brad/*

Following Jesus into Eternal Life.
Contact: ryderwrite@cox.net